VIRTUAL COLLECTIONS IN DIGITAL LIBRARIES

Vibhuti Agarwal

RAJAT PUBLICATIONS
New Delhi

Virtual Collections in Digital Libraries
by *Vibhuti Agarwal*

This edition is published by Rajat Publications
4740/23, Ansari Road Daryaganj,
New Delhi - 110002

ISBN: 978-81-7880-257-2

Edition 2025

Rs. 2295/-

Printed and bound in India

RAJAT
PUBLICATIONS

4740/23, Ansari Road, Daryaganj,
New Delhi- 110002 (India)
Mob:- +91-9811484973, +91-9811105389
E-mail: rajat_publication@yahoo.com

Preface

Digital libraries are a set of electronic resources and associated technical capabilities for creating, searching, and using information. They are an extension and enhancement of information storage and retrieval systems that manipulate digital data in any medium and exist in distributed networks. Almost all digital libraries are made up of a number of virtual elements including the internet and intranets; integrated access to information; digitisation of materials; access to electronic publications; electronic document delivery; resource sharing; cooperative developments; and, end-user services.

A digital library that contains virtual collections helps its users in several ways. A new user who may be intimidated by a digital library's search interface or the number of results returned by a query might be better introduced to the digital library through the more easily explorable partitioned set of resources in a virtual collection. A directory of the virtual collections contained by a digital library, can provide a good introduction and overview of the library's contents to new or casual users.

Associating resources with virtual collections enables those resources to be found more easily, either by browsing the contents of a highlighted virtual collection or through standard search and browse interfaces. Adding virtual collections to search facilities enables a user to perform a standard search but restrict it to a specific virtual collection, which could provide a more manageable and higher-quality result set than by searching the entire digital library.

The benefits of virtual collections do not come without a price, of course. For a digital library to be able to easily create and remove virtual collections, to associate resources with different virtual collections in a flexible way, and to help users find and use the virtual collections, the library must have a structured approach to representing these collections. Moreover, to make creating such collections practical, this approach should also strive to minimise the costs associated with creating virtual collections.

This book introduce the concept of virtual collections and outline the costs and benefits for defining such collections. It discusses the implications of virtual collections for enhancing interoperability and sharing across digital libraries. Students and professionals of library and information science will benefit from the contents of the book.

Editor

Contents

Contents

1
Virtual Library

A virtual library is the way a traditional library uses technology and innovation to meet customer demand, and that the common thread is the "use of technology to improve customer delivery, as well as the search and retrieval technology available on electronic networks". Five common elements for digital libraries are as following:

— The digital library is not a single entity;

— The digital library requires technology to link with the resources of the many;

— The linkages between the many digital libraries and information services are transparent to the end users;

— Universal access to digital libraries and information services is a goal; and,

— Digital library collections are not limited to document surrogates: they extend to digital artefacts that cannot be represented or distributed in printed formats.

The virtual library may also be called the library without walls, digital library, electronic library, e-library, desktop library, online library, future library, library of the future, logical library, networked library, hybrid library, gateway library, extended library or information superhighway. Of these many terms, virtual library, digital library, hybrid library and electronic (or e-) library are most common.

Model of Virtual Library

Virtual libraries may be made up of a number of components, including: the Internet and Intranets; integrated access to information; digitisation of materials; access to electronic publications; electronic document delivery; resource sharing; cooperative developments; and, end-user services. These elements, then, may be considered the basic building blocks of the virtual library, although the nature and extent of the application of each component will depend upon the circumstances and needs of the library and/or organisation to which the virtual library is attached. One basic virtual library model may then be illustrated as shown in Figure 1.

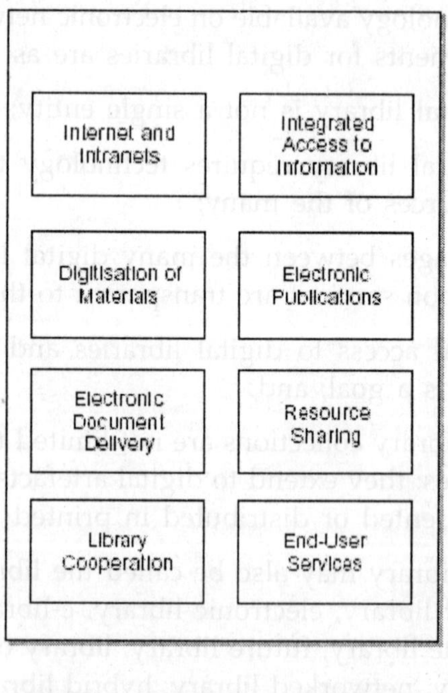

Figure 1. Virtual library components

The development of virtual libraries appears to be heavily dependent on a number of inter-related enabling (or hindering) factors, comprising: legal issues; financial issues; client issues; personnel issues; organisational issues; management issues; technological issues; collaboration issues; and, subject discipline issues. Although writers in the field differ on the importance of the individual issues, it is widely agreed that continued progress and ultimate success of virtual libraries is dependent on their resolution. If this is the case, then these issues make up an environment that surrounds the virtual library itself. This may be modelled as shown in Figure 2.

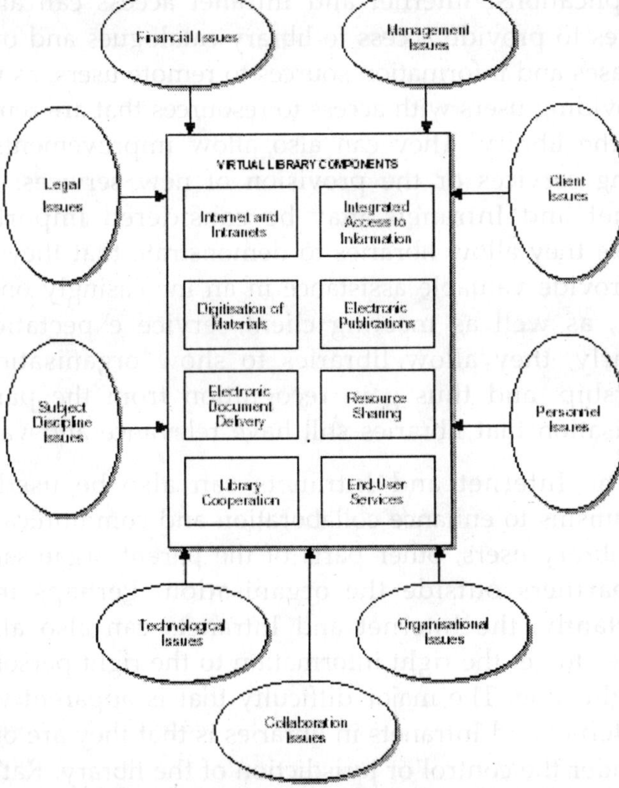

Figure 2. Virtual libraries and their environment

Virtual Library Components

The literature on the topic shows that virtual libraries can be made up of a number of complementary and inter-related components. Given the relative lack of balance in the literature, it is often not clear what the application, importance, and issues/problems with each component may be, however, a synthesis of the available information suggests the following.

Internet and Intranets

Libraries may use the Internet and Intranets for a variety of applications. Internet and Intranet access can allow libraries to provide access to library catalogues and other databases and information sources to remote users, as well as providing users with access to resources that are remote from the library. They can also allow improvements to existing services or the provision of new services. The Internet and Intranets may be considered important because they allow libraries to demonstrate that they can still provide valuable assistance in an increasingly online world, as well as meeting client service expectations. Similarly, they allow libraries to show organisational leadership, and thus gain recognition from the parent organisation that libraries still have relevance and value.

The Internet and Intranets can also be used as mechanisms to enhance collaboration and communication with library users, other parts of the parent organisation and partners outside the organisation. Perhaps most importantly, the Internet and Intranets can also allow libraries to get the right information to the right person at the right time. The major difficulty that is apparent with the Internet and Intranets in libraries is that they are often not under the control or jurisdiction of the library. Rather, they tend to be controlled by information technology areas, or by multi-functional teams led by information technology areas. This means that it can be difficult for libraries to gain best advantage from their Internet and Intranet applications.

Integrated Access to Information

Integrated access to information falls into two areas: enhancements to OPACs, and the use of a single workstation to access multiple electronic resources. Catalogue enhancements can include the incorporation of other libraries' holdings within a local OPAC, a gateway facility to external library catalogues, and/or a search facility incorporating multiple library catalogues. Single workstation access can allow the use of multiple resources through a single access point.

Integrated access to information is significant because it provides users with a single starting point for internal and external searching. Likewise, access to many resources can be combined through an integrated front end, promoting ease of use. In effect, it provides users with a "one-stop shop" resource discovery facility. There are, however, several issues relating to integrated access that must be considered. Full integration can be difficult, because information sources from different suppliers use differing, often proprietary, formats and standards, making it difficult to fully integrate them into a single front-end. This is equally true of library OPACs, which are usually sourced from different suppliers, by different libraries.

There are also issues with the incorporation of an external library's materials into a local OPAC, as it could be argued that it is neither efficient nor effective to use scarce staff resources to add external holdings to a local catalogue. If external materials are made searchable, through whatever means, there is also an issue relating to whether the searched materials can be obtained by local clients.

Materials Digitisation

Digitisation of hard-copy materials has two major applications in virtual libraries. It can be used to create a body of electronic full-text material for client use. It is also valuable in allowing "special" collections, such as manuscripts, maps, photographs, or historically significant or rare materials to be made available. The importance of digitisation lies in the fact that libraries can create a body of material that clients like, and want to use, in turn allowing them to be better satisfied. There are also advantages in relation to remote access to materials, wherever and whenever a client wishes to access them.

In the area of special collections, digitisation allows materials that would not normally be widely accessible to clients to be made accessible. This has the dual advantage of making rich research materials available to a much wider community, while allowing the better preservation of the hard-copy resource. There are several difficulties to be overcome by digitisation programmes. There is far too much hard-copy material in existence for all of it to be scanned and made available electronically, so strategic decisions must be made about what will and will not be digitised. It is likewise a time-consuming and resource intensive process to scan the selected materials.

The scanned materials are often quite large computer files, which places heavy demands on technology capabilities and data storage requirements. It can also be difficult to obtain permission from rightsowners to digitise their copyrighted materials. Even when permission can be obtained, licensing fees can be prohibitive, and the limitations placed on usage can be too restrictive to be practical.

Electronic Publications

Electronic publications can be divided into two distinct groups: electronic journals and electronic full-text. However, the application of the two forms is quite similar, and in many respects, the application and usage of these materials mirrors that of their hard-copy counterparts. Nevertheless, there are some significant advantages to the use of electronic publications over their paper equivalents. The importance of electronic publications is that they tend to allow greater flexibility of access to materials, which is critical in the virtual library environment. They can allow remote access, and access at any time, day or night.

Likewise, they can allow simultaneous access by multiple users, and can permit linking between one part of a publication and another, or indeed, between different publications. They also eliminate the problem of missing, late or stolen documents, and the need for binding of materials. Despite this, there remain some significant problems to be overcome. There is not yet a critical mass of electronic publications available, making complete conversion to electronic publications problematic. There are also major issues relating to the purchase of such materials, including pricing, copyright, archiving, access/usage restrictions by publishers, continued access to already purchased materials when subscriptions are cancelled, preservation, and integration of electronic resources from multiple suppliers.

Electronic Document Delivery

The actual application of electronic document delivery is basically no different from its hard-copy equivalent. However, increasing client expectations and decreasing resources have created a much greater reliance on resource sharing in the electronic era. The importance of electronic document delivery is that it can be used to maintain adequate and rapid access to resources not held locally, in an era of rising costs and declining budgets. The major issue that affects electronic document delivery is that it needs to minimise the time delay between request and delivery to be useful.

Library clients are unlikely to be satisfied with the service offered if electronic document delivery methods do not take less time than traditional hard-copy delivery. The other issue to be resolved in this area is the impact that copyright has, whether on digitisation of existing paper-based materials or the supply of materials that are 'born digital'.

Resource Sharing

The importance of resource sharing in virtual libraries is several-fold. Consortial approaches allow participants to share costs, while maintaining access to resources, with such approaches often favoured by funding bodies. Given the variety of formats and technologies currently available, there are now many ways of providing access to information—having resources located onsite is only one. Library users generally want to be able to access information, regardless of location and source, and resource sharing fits this model. There are four main problems inherent in resource sharing models.

Where resource sharing arrangements have not been formally created (that is, libraries simply rely on others to maintain their holdings of a particular resource), there is an assumption that a discontinued resource will continue to be held by someone else, which may or may not be true. Also, most libraries are likely to be unwilling to lend their rare, valuable or unique materials or items in very high demand. There is also a need to balance local needs with consortial needs; a consortial arrangement that requires libraries to put consortial requirements ahead of local users is unlikely to be sustainable. Likewise, consortial arrangements require strong policy frameworks to be workable in practice.

Cooperative Developments

Cooperative developments may encompass two main strands, these being cooperative development or purchase of software tools by a number of partners, and joint purchase or development of hardware and other computer technologies. This is particularly relevant to high-use, high-demand materials, as these are generally what libraries want to share. Cooperative development is becoming important through sheer necessity. It is undeniable that digital resources are expensive, and there are usually no new budget allocations for libraries to purchase or develop electronic resources.

To take advantage of what the digital environment has to offer, libraries therefore need to expand cooperation. There are several problems that can impede cooperative developments, however. Local priorities can be treated as more important, effectively undermining the cooperative arrangement. There can also be unwillingness by participants to cede local autonomy and authority. Geographic location can cause problems in administration and development, especially where participants are widespread. Where joint purchase of commercial sources is proposed, there can be reluctance on the part of rightsowners to permit sharing.

End-User Services

End-user services in the virtual library environment covers three main elements: end-user access to online tools and electronic full-text, end-user search training, and the facility for direct user requesting of materials. Libraries are tending to offer end-user access to materials because, in the electronic era, users have the expectation of access to materials, in full-text, and on their desktop.

Direct requesting is usually applied in the form of loan and inter-library loan functions, often using email and/or the Internet. In terms of access to materials, users who are able to access resources themselves are advantaged over those who cannot, both in terms of the tools available to them, and the times and places at which they are available. End-user requesting is advantageous because users perceive that external materials do not cost them any greater effort to obtain than local ones, and there is a perception that the process has been made faster. In each case, users are empowered, while library staff can devote time that used to be spent on processing to other matters.

Again, there are several difficulties inherent in end-user services. There are policy implications for what people can and cannot have access to, circulation policies, loan periods, borrowing limits, and other related matters. Likewise, libraries that participate in such schemes need to show commitment to consortial users, not just local users. There is also a danger of wasteful and/or malicious requesting. User support and training must also be increased in the electronic environment, so that clients can effectively use the services that have been put in place.

Virtual Library Environment

Surrounding the virtual library itself are a number of inter-related issues, which directly impact on the extent to which virtual libraries can be successfully developed. Unfortunately, the literature on the topic does not give an overall view of these issues. There is also a lack of balance in the literature, with some issues, especially in the areas of law and technology, receiving much attention, while other, equally important, issues are only covered in a very minimal or superficial way.

Virtual Services

Original concept of a digital or virtual library evolved from a view that electronic information storage and access was the full scope of service for the new library. The original perspectives of a service oriented to files and 'resource discovery' based on file naming and retrieval algorithms. In describing the development of the concept of a digital library the underlying service model can provide information on assumptions made about the roles of library users and librarians.

The role of reference in digital or virtual libraries can be explored, based on both the original concepts and taking into account lessons learnt for reference in the printed library and the digital. The early concepts of a digital library were based on a 'seamless' automated access to information without traditional reference services. For example among the definitions of a "digital library" are:

- The digital library is not a single entity;
- The digital library requires technology to link the resources of many;
- The linkages between the many digital libraries and information services are transparent to the end users;
- Universal access to digital libraries and information services is a goal;
- Digital library collections are not limited to document surrogates: they extend to digital artifacts that cannot be represented or distributed in printed formats.

Purposes of a North American digital library system are:

— to expedite the systematic development of: the means to collect, store, and organise information and knowledge in digital form; and of digital library collections in North America;

— to promote the economical and efficient delivery of information to all sectors of North American society;

— to encourage co-operative efforts which leverage the considerable investment in North American research resources, computing and communications network;

— to strengthen communication and collaboration between and among the research, business, government, and educational communities;

— to take an international leadership role in the generation and dissemination of knowledge in areas of strategic importance to North America;

— to contribute to the lifelong learning opportunities of all North Americans.

Hybrid libraries can also be seen as located on a continuum between the conventional and digital library, where electronic and paper-based information sources are used alongside each other. The challenge associated with the management of the hybrid library is to encourage end-user resource discovery and information use, in a variety of formats and from a number of local and remote sources, in a seamlessly integrated way. The hybrid library should be "designed to bring a range of technologies from different sources together in the context of a working library, and also to begin to explore integrated systems and services in both the electronic and print environments."

The hybrid library should not, then, be seen as nothing more than an uneasy transitional phase between the conventional library and digital library but, rather, as a worthwhile model in its own right, which can be usefully developed and improved. This model contains the natural reference librarian for the print world, allows for the existence of a 'Cybrarian' for the electronic environment but does not yet have a multi-skilled reference service at its core. Some of the definitions which appeared after this evolution in thinking include Paul Duguid who described a digital library as "an environment to bring together collections, services, and people in support of the full life cycle of creation, dissemination, use, and preservation of data, information and knowledge".

A full understanding of the role of reference is emerging now but a well-developed service model is still to be articulated. The concepts embedded in the hybrid library and emerging knowledge management field offer the greatest insights at present. To explore the nature of reference librarianship in the digital or hybrid library explores two perspectives—that of the users or clients and that of the library. The differences and similarities in the expectations of these two groups give an indication of how reference services can operate in the digital environment. They also provide a context for the trials of difference services, which are occurring in the National Library of Australia and in collaborative projects.

Three online services—electronic reference enquiry approaches within the library and two collaborative approaches are then assessed against the expectations and as possible service models.

Digital Reference

In research libraries such as the National Library of Australia users had been provided with reference services in mediated and unmediated transactions. In the print library mediated transactions are the face to face reference enquiries well described in library literature and for which the basic skills have been a core unit in library studies through the professions history. Unmediated reference occurs with the use of tools produced by libraries to enable users to access information or undertake their library research.

Guides for readers, such as Pathfinders to subjects, information sheets on searching for types of materials such as journal articles, finding aids for manuscript collections and documentation on searching have been produced to enable users to research effectively. They have been a key component in the information literacy programmes of libraries, in some cases being the only part of information literacy or training programmes that have been available in all the hours that the library is open. In the networked environment libraries have make guides and pathfinders available online, often integrated with digital resource lists, such as at the National Library and in OCLC's CORC project. This first stage of evolution of digital self-help or unmediated reference was a natural first step. Guides were already in electronic form, generally as word processing documents and had been tested with the user population and developed over many years.

Mediated reference enquiries in the digital world are those which are expressed in electronic form. The most commonly used methods are email or web form, now widely available in research libraries. All Australian State libraries and the National Library have web forms and email reference services, in the National Library's case dating back to 1994. Research into use of the digital reference service indicates a significant uptake of this medium for transmitting reference enquiries. As an example the increase in electronic reference enquiries shows a consistent pattern.

For unmediated reference services general web site statistics show a steady increase. Differentiating reference products from the web site in general has commenced with detailed report available through products such as Webtrends. For example, the National Library's Reference and Newspaper pages are in the top 3 directly accessed. The Australian newspapers and Newspapers home page are accessed over 10,000 times per month.

In understanding digital reference needs of users librarians have been able to take account of research into user needs in mediated on-site reference. There are some major differences in the patterns of enquiries electronically, as well as some differences in characteristics in the networked environment. Perhaps the most obvious is the nature of the users relationship to the library. When users had to physically visit or write to a library they had a relatively clear understanding of the role of the particular library and their relationship with it.

If they were studying at a campus the educational nature of their information needs was relatively obvious in their use of the academic library. In a research library the visible collection gave a strong presentation indicating the subject interest of the organisation. Users visiting the library in various organisations were explicitly reminded of the nature and purpose of the library, through location, signage and collections. Users have experienced library services through a number of different facets of their life. The fact that many users used a wide range of libraries because of the distribution of collections has been well established.

While many users visit a range of research and academic libraries to support their on-going information needs, others had different roles with various libraries. In a typical example a user may work in an agency and use that library for work related research, be studying at an academic institution and use that library for their study, use the National Library to supplement other libraries both for academic and work related research and use the local public library for recreation as well as supplementing study materials.

Users may well in the print world have 'belonged': from the library point of view to 4 or 5 or more libraries, segmenting their use through visits. The concept of 'My library' is then a network of libraries, each different and potentially confusing. A networked environment allows a different perspective to be taken to library services. The clues that exist in the physical library to orient users and make clear the services and collections available are much more elusive and complex in the electronic environment. Users also have the opportunity for an immediacy of service, which means their interaction is effectively 'seamless'.

In this model reference service is on tap, clearly visible with a turnaround time of minutes rather than hours. For virtual library services clients are required to navigate around library web sites. The challenge of determining the details of subject, geographic and temporal coverage of the library's collection and knowledge is significant. While the organisations name may give some clues, particularly if the user is a student or on the staff of an organisation, different knowledge is required to use each library's web site.

'Seamless' service may exist in any one library's web site but for a user navigating through more than one library the result is very far from seamless. To assess the needs of users both in the networked and print library environment a series of focus groups were conducted at the National Library from July to September 2000. The three groups comprised of post-graduate humanities students from the Australian National University,

Petherick Reading Room Readers and members of the Independent Scholars Association of Australia.

The key comments made in focus groups were that users wish to access a mix of print and electronic resources with a new reference service. Traditional mediated reference services answering enquires are seen by the users canvassed as not as critical as they have been. Rather, users expect the reference service to provide them with the skills and knowledge to be able to search effectively themselves in the networked environment. Users recognise that this is very complex and requires constant work because of the changing (and increasing) resources available.

Additional complexity is added by the fact that individual libraries offer access through different interfaces, offer different full text and indexes and have different degrees of coverage of their collections in electronic catalogues. Users expect libraries to offer 'one stop shop', however they recognise that different resources and reference services are provided depending upon the nature of the library. The time required to retrain and reorient for each library was seen as a significant impediment to effective research.

Unmediated reference services together with training emerged as the Cinderellas of reference service in a networked environment. Training, particularly for users inexperienced in the use of computers and also for those accessing new resources. Training was seen as essentially a face to face service in small groups, partly as this facilitates self paced learning and offers flexibility. Information literacy programmes based on either automated or online tutorials or rigid programmes were considered to be of only limited use. Unmediated online reference services such as lists of resources and guides to library research were seen as very valuable as they could be accessed anywhere, anytime.

In summary, users expressed a desire to access resources, both library collections and tools to assist their research 24 hours per day in the situation of greatest convenience. Many users study late at night and wish to work effectively without requiring mediated reference services at this time. However, there does remain a need for mediated reference services in training and answering library research enquires. Counterbalancing this is the experience of the National Library in email and webform enquires. These enquires suggest that for many Australians information is now thought of as completely digital and freely available.

They expect library staff to provide resources directly. They appear to have lost an understanding of the library research process and the need to structure enquires for persistent searching. The new model of digital libraries incorporating information literary skills and services requires a long term programme to develop the knowledge of our users. Matching library user and library expectations for digital reference reveals some gaps in perceptions. The main differences are:

Library User Perceptions	Library perception
'Belong' to many users	See users as 'belonging' to that library
Experience information needs anywhere at anytime	See interactions on web site (resource access and unmediated reference) and in library 'space/ hours' in mediated reference
Not dependant on individual products but seek aggregated tailored access	Structure information by details of each component eg. Title, publisher

Digital Reference Models

In the print world libraries answered reference enquires form their collection, the knowledge of library staff and the network of contacts or other libraries developed over years. The principles of such a reference service include a recognition of the role or scope of each library, defined relationships with other libraries; knowledge of the collection strengths and a commensurate knowledge of the strengths of library staff. While these principles apply in the digital environment the potential scope of collections with Internet access is vast.

Users may also come from communities not previously served buy the library, but for whom Internet access has enabled the breaking of boundaries of geographic or knowledge isolation. These complex issues have led to the development of collaborative models of digital reference services. These models can build upon the distributed strengths of libraries and their ready connectivity.

Some of the models that have emerged can be seen in the Collaborative Digital Reference Service; State/ National Library Cooperation; CORC and subject portals. The National Library is participating in an initiative developed by the Library of Congress, the Collaborative Digital Reference Service. The participants are taking part in a pilot project to test the provision of professional library-quality reference service to users any time anywhere through an international digital network of libraries.

Phase 1 took place from February to March 2000. The goals were build a system with information on the subject strengths and availability hours of participating libraries for online reference, to enable routing and management of reference enquiries. To help build these profiles all libraries, including the National Library, contributed some general reference enquiries and answers, to indicate their subject strengths. A web inquiry form has been constructed and tested.

In phase 2, due to commence in July, further work will be done with the software including more robust testing of automated routing of inquiries, workflow issues, statistics and benefits of using the service. This phase will include referring current inquiries asked of member libraries to other libraries and will end in August 2000. Administrative issues including legal issues, staff training and service level agreements will begin to be resolved.

Phase 3, will enable detailed evaluation to take place. During this phase will take inquiries from patrons and will 'stress test' the model, service levels, performance, costs, benefits and management/governance issues. The project aim is for participant libraries with branch or other local libraries share the answering of reference enquiries based on their areas of expertise, aiming in the long run for 24 hours a day 7 days a week online reference services. A conceptual model of the service is:

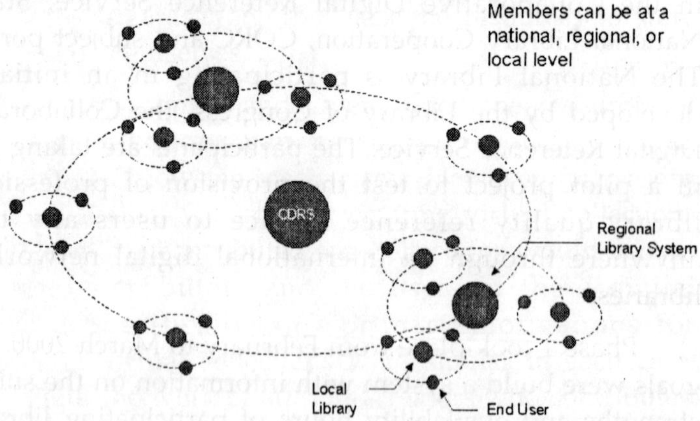

Participants in phase 1 and 2 the project include:

Library of Congress	Peninsula Library System (San Francisco area)
Cornell University Library (USA)	National Agricultural
University of Texas, Austin	National Library of
Canada	
Santa Monica Public Library	National Library of
Australia	
Morris County Public Library	Smithsonian American Art Museum

Co-operative Online Research Catalog (CORC)

In 1998 the largest American supplier of bibliographic records, OCLC, announced it would work on the development of a Co-operative Online Research Catalog project. The project comprised 2 parts—first a catalogue of Internet resources, to which the National Library contributed records from Kinetica and secondly a mechanism to share guides to help readers identify Internet resources, material held in library collections and databases primarily based on subjects.

An example of a guide that produce which would be usefully shared with other libraries is 'Australian literature on the Internet'. This guide is of great interest to American universities offering course in Australian and New Zealand Studies. During the pilot phase the National Library tested 3 guides through the Pathfinder system. Consultations are continuing about the publication of guides on CORC. From 1 July 2000 the Internet resources catalogue component of CORC has become a production system, with a new charging schedule. The pathfinder project has yet to reach a successful technical architecture. The National Library produced a report on CORC pathfinders in late 1999 suggesting some development directions that would improve the effectiveness and efficiency.

The University of New South Wales Library also conducted an extensive evaluation and produced a report, which identified similar strengths and weaknesses in CORC. OCLC have indicated they will be reinvestigating pathfinders after the launch of the CORC database, and have developed a proposed list of enhancements based to a large extent on our recommendations. The Council of Australian State Libraries approved the establishment of a Working Group on Reference Issues at its June 2000 meeting, and discussed the possible role of such a group.

The National Library is chairing this group. The draft terms of reference are to identify issues in which a collaborative approach will result in better reference services in Australian libraries. Major issues include working towards an Australian library reference collection and virtual reference services. The group will also investigate developments such as call centre technology, and discuss reader research and reference needs, benchmarking and staff competencies.

Membership includes Reference Managers from all state and territory libraries and the National Library. Priorities for 2000 include collaborative work on reference tools, such as reader guides and Internet guides. The benefits of the project will be to enhance access to this information though creation of Australian library guides to resources covering all states and territories and also in reduce the duplication of work done in each library on these guides. A model of the potential shape of the service follows:

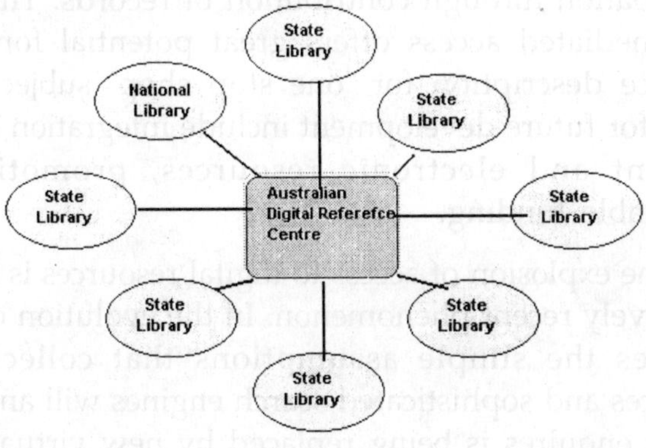

This service initiative has potential to provide an Australian node for the Collaborative Digital Reference Service. It should also provide a model for sharing pathfinders to contribute to CORC.

Subject gateways: A concept of subject access to electronic information has been developed in a new form with the introduction subject portals or gateways. These aim to enable access to resources within a defined area, forming the next generation of tools, a step up from the resource discovery tools of enthusiastic researchers or amateurs.The fundamental purposes of the information portals are:

— Provide for convenient and effective access to information resources (most often Internet resources) through a single gateway

— Description of resources according to agreed standards after selection for quality and subject content

— Identification of information resources to agreed content guidelines (most often subject areas such as agriculture or chemistry).

The National Library has been involved in the development of technical and policy advice and in participation through contribution of records. This model of unmediated access offers great potential for sharing resource description for 'one stop shop' subject access. Issues for future development include integration of access to print and electronic resources, promotion and sustainable funding.

The explosion of access to digital resources is however a relatively recent phenomenon. In the evolution of digital libraries the simple assumptions that collections of resources and sophisticated search engines will answer the worlds enquires is being replaced by new virtual service models. Collaboration appears to be the key for effective use of information services, both mediated and unmediated. The experiments of CDRS, CORC, Australian co-operation and subject portals provide defined individual projects to test these new models.

In looking for future directions, forthcoming evaluations and consideration of how the projects could be amalgamated into larger combined services will be the next steps. Major issues including the role of the National Bibliographic Database, a possible Australian metadata repository and knowledge management system to create access to implicit knowledge need to be addressed. In all of these the National Library and other Australian libraries need to continue to actively debate tools and services.

Some major Issues, which related to the virtual libraries are described below.

Legal Issues

The legal issues surrounding virtual libraries can be divided into two areas, that are given below:

— copyright and related matters, and
— privacy.

Copyright has the potential to impact of virtual library development in a very direct and profound way. There is a threat that virtual libraries can be totally derailed, as rightsowners want current protections to be increased. At the same time, libraries and library users wish the current exemptions, such as fair dealing, to continue in a digital environment. It is perhaps inevitable that current copyright laws will be adapted in the electronic environment, as paper-based models may not be appropriate.

In any case, both rightsowners and users have legitimate concerns, and it is important for the success of digital libraries that reformed copyright laws balance the ability of users to access materials at a reasonable price, while bringing reasonable returns to rightsowners, in order to stimulate further production. It is already apparent that large amounts of data about individuals can be collected in the digital arena; data that the individual may not know exists. In many respects, the increased use of technology exacerbates privacy risks. This leads to new responsibilities for librarians to safeguard the privacy of their users, for while rightsholders need to track the usage of their materials, users need to be protected. Again, current laws are not particularly suited to the realities of the digital environment, and require updating to accommodate them.

Financial Issues

Financial issues are likely to impact the extent to which libraries are able to move to digital models. Complete costs are hard to determine, but it seems unlikely that great savings will exist in a digital environment. Materials may well become cheaper to produce, but the technologies required to support them will doubtless be more extensive and complex, and thus, more expensive. It also seems likely that more fee-for-service and metered usage models will be used by content suppliers, although working out who owes what to whom is likely to be difficult, due to the sheer scale of information, parties and transactions involved.

Given current constraints on library budgets, it is improbable that there will be large amounts of 'new' money available to pay for electronic developments, so constraints on the amount and types of available services seem likely. Given these factors, and the fact that virtual libraries will be a long-term and ongoing cost, not a one-off add-on, libraries will need to formulate budget strategies to address these issues.

Client Issues

User needs must be treated as paramount if virtual libraries are to work. This is because, on the one hand, user expectations have increased in the electronic environment—perhaps more than libraries can deliver, while on the other, client resistance can potentially delay or derail virtual library development, either partially or totally. Library users must therefore be incorporated in system design, so that the available mix of materials and services offered fits both their information needs and information seeking practices.

Personnel Issues

Although the human resource implications are not entirely clear, it seems obvious that the duties, and therefore the skills, of library staff will also change as existing services are altered to become more electronic and new digital services are created. It is quite likely that core competencies will be much more 'technologically' based than might previously have been the case. As duties and responsibilities change, training and development needs for library staff will be similarly altered. The ongoing computerisation of libraries also carries with it the potential for deskilling and/or deprofessionalisation of library staff, which in turn requires librarians to justify their ongoing claim to professional status.

Organisational Issues

Just as library staff will need to make changes in the virtual library environment, so too will organisational structures change. Technology is creating new jobs while eliminating others, and traditional divisions between functional areas are likely to be much reduced or entirely eliminated. Similarly, the mix of library staff needed (professional to paraprofessional) is altering, and the duties performed by the various levels of staff are also shifting. It is difficult to know to what extent organisational size will impact on successful virtual library development, given the apparent disagreement of the literature in this area. However, it is a factor that merits consideration. Overall, organisational structures will need to be less rigid, reflecting the fluid nature of the changing library environment.

Management Issues

In order to accomplish virtual library goals, there are a number of management issues that libraries must consider. Libraries will need better strategic planning than has previously been the case, as it will be impossible to reach virtual library goals if these are not known. Alongside this stands a need for sound financial planning. There will likewise be a need for better performance measurement and statistical measures, as current measures are unlikely to gather all the data that will need to be recorded in a virtual library environment. Perhaps most importantly of all, there will be a critical need for leadership within libraries, as virtual libraries are likely to cause ongoing, perhaps unprecedented change. There will also be a need for libraries to show leadership to their parent organisations, so that they are prepared to adopt new technologies and new ways of dealing with information.

Technological Issues

Technological issues will obviously have a major impact on whether or not virtual libraries can succeed. In this area, there are several major issues that must be considered. One critical need is for 'properly' functioning and stable systems—if the supporting technologies fail or are unreliable, then virtual library access and useability will be partially or totally compromised. For optimum effectiveness and useability, there is also need for seamless integration of the technologies and digitised materials, supported by appropriate legal and policy developments, as well as technological standards. Another challenge is the rapidly changing technology environment; for virtual libraries to be successful, the dual issues of technological change and technological obsolescence must be properly addressed, and sound data migration and preservation plans put in place.

Collaboration Issues

It is clear that the sheer volume of materials, systems and issues involved make it impossible for a single library to stand alone in the virtual library environment. In order to succeed, partnerships will need to be created, with users, other libraries, and information creators and suppliers. Given the very technological nature of virtual libraries, closer relationships are also likely to be needed with computer centres and information technology experts. It is often thought that libraries will need to create mechanisms to support cooperation, or they will not survive in an era where end-users can obtain much of the information they require without going through library intermediaries.

Subject Discipline Issues

The success of virtual libraries also depends to an extent on libraries' subject specialities. It is quite apparent that when it comes to the availability of electronic content, the material available for the different subject disciplines varies enormously, both in terms of quantity and quality. It is also clear that digital developments are being supported and adopted to differing extents by people within the disciplinary communities, as the needs of the disciplines can vary greatly. Until recently, the computer science community largely set the virtual library agenda, and other disciplinary viewpoints and needs were not necessarily given much consideration. This also impacts on the success of virtual library development.

2

Creating Virtual Library

Whereas a decade ago, the state of the art in a research area could be found out by reading conference proceedings and journals in the local library, nowadays it is additionally necessary to find these electronic publications on the web. Traditional search engines do not help for this task, because they do not index e.g. postscript documents, which is the electronic format of many preprints appearing on the web.

The few existing searchable indices for postscript documents either cover too large fields—all of computer science, for example—to be really helpful, or they depend on some submission procedure which delays the appearance of the documents on the web. A searchable index for scientific papers which is specialised in a relatively small research area and also allows to find the latest new documents.

This proceeds in three steps. In the first step, a list of names of people who are active in the research under consideration is constructed. This information is obtained from electronic computer science bibliographies, and therefore the names found can be seen as "certified." In the second step, the Home Pages of these people are found. In the third step, these Home Pages are used as starting points for a search engine, which collects scientific papers in the area close to these Home Pages.

Figure 1. Creation of a virtual library

The documents are used to create a searchable index which is accessible on a web server.

HPSearch

HPSearch is a web-based, topic-oriented information system for finding and watching scientifically relevant personal Home Pages. Personal Home Pages have obtained an important position in scientific communication. Preprints and long versions of published papers, project descriptions, course material and contact information can be found there.

HPSearch shows two advantages in comparison to standard search engines:

— System has collect a large amount of topic-specific data. The Home Pages of 75,000 scientists were searched. Their names are mainly provided by the DBLP.

— HPSearch has built up a domain-specific knowledge.

HPSearch works as follows: A set of candidate Home Pages is formed with the help of usual search engines. Each page is rated and a ranking is built. The highest rated candidate Home Pages are visited by an agent and are rated again, a final ranking is built. The result is stored in a database.

The user queries HPSearch by a Web-interface (Figure 2) and receives a hypertext-view of the results. He has also the possibility to start a Web search if the name is not in the database. HPSearch is implemented in Java. In order to maintain the information content the results are reconsidered regularly.

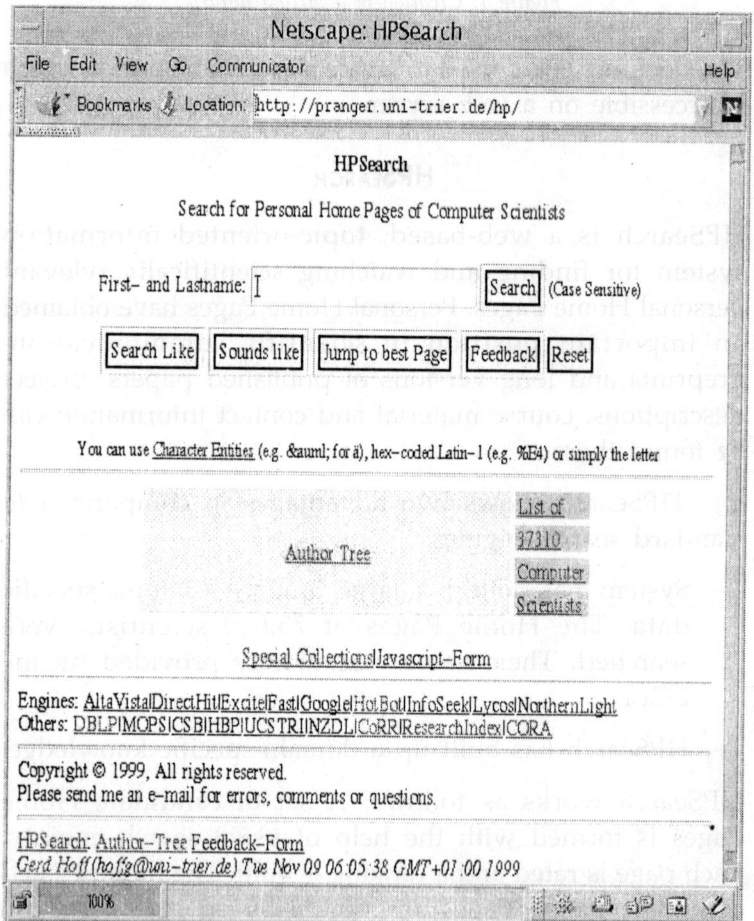

Figure 2. Start page of HPSearch

Now, we can see personal Home Pages, rating function and ranking, maintenance of information , architecture of the system, working plan of the search and experiences.

Personal Home Pages

A scientifical personal Home Page is a hypertext page (actually in HTML) which is created by the scientist himself or by his order. Its main function is to present users an overview over his work. The classification of hypertext pages and especially the identification of personal Home Pages is a difficult task. There are not any fixed rules which describe scientists' personal Home Pages.

We determine characteristics with the help of a set of training documents (reference set). These hypertext pages are known as personal Home Pages of computer scientists. A second set of pages (which is determined by the results of the search engines) is used for control (control set). Both sets have a size of 1,000 elements. A characteristic C has to be both

— relevant, a certain percentage R of documents in the reference set have it, and

— significant, the ratio

— percentage of documents with the characteristic C in the reference set

— percentage of documents with the characteristic C in the control set

— has a certain value.

Experiences shows that expedient values are R = 2.5 % and S = 2. Here obtain about 500 such characteristics and highlight the most important facts:

— The probability that certain words appear in different sections on the page is very different and find out that it is reasonable to distinguish the sections title, first header-tag on a page, all other header-tags, labels from links, and other text within a HTML-page. For example the word publications appears in 0.2 % (2.3 %) in the title, 0.7 % (1.0 %) in the first header, 12.2 % (1.4 %) in other headers, 25.4 % (3.4 %) in labels and 16.6 % (5.5 %) in other text in the reference set.

— The name of the person is mostly found in title (89.8 % versus 20.0 % in control set), first header (51.0 % vs. 4.8 %) or URL (44.0 % vs. 3.0 %).
— The "~" -character (65.5 %) or strings like "people" appear (in combination with the name) in the URL.
— There are references to his publications.
— The size of a personal Home Pages is small. The median size in the reference set is 3KB, in the control set it is 9KB.

The domain-specific knowledge itself is changing permanently too. A comparable test from May 5, 1997 shows for example that 46.0 % of the documents have a "~"-character in the URL. Therefore we repeat the above procedure every month automatically.

Rating Function

From the characteristics worked out, a 2-step rating function is formed. Rating function instead of classical text classification algorithms like naive Bayes, nearest neighbour or decision trees because of the following reasons:

— The structure of the document is hard to handle with pure text classification.
— The number of characteristics is too high.

— We rate some off-the-page criteria (e.g. URL-structure, search engine provided information, links from other Web-pages).

— In the first step of the search, we do not have the entire document.

— Everything in the system including the rating criteria is highly dynamic. With the automatic update-able rating function the system keeps implementable.

— Since there is a query term, the name of the person searched for, our application is no pure classification problem.

In step 1, HPSearch evaluates the entries received by the search engines: Title, URL, description and position made by search engines ranking algorithms are made available.

After creating a first ranking (presorting), HPSearch reads the best candidate Home Pages, whereby header, links, meta-tags and normal text are evaluated (step 2). A final ranking is built.

Maintaining of Information

Maintaining of information is a primary task of HPSearch. High actuality must be kept. Therefore HPSearch has two parametrically controllable mechanisms which work periodically and event-oriented. Evaluation of DBLP access-logs: Daily, HPSearch evaluates the access-logs of the person pages in DBLP. Names unknown to HPSearch or names for which the search took place a long time ago are searched for. In a middle-sized time period, a function which depends on the date of search and the score of the best page decides whether a search is started or not. This direct interconnection to the access-log of DBLP guarantees that the data collected by HPSearch is up-to-date.

parameter: SEARCHDAYS1, SEARCHDAYS2 with SEARCHDAYS1 < SEARCHDAYS2
input: name of a person
output: startSearch (search will be started)

```
IF        (name not in HPSearch )
          startSearch = true
ELSEIF    (days since last search > SEARCHDAYS2)
          startSearch = true
ELSEIF    (days since last search < SEARCHDAYS1)
          startSearch = false
ELSE      startSearch = f(days since last search, best score)
```

Validation of URLs

Weekly, HPSearch checks for each name the URL of the best rated page on existence. Each URL is checked at least twice before it is removed from the HPSearch -database. Then HPSearch starts a new search for that name.

parameter: CHECKDAYS1, CHECKDAYS2 with CHECKDAYS2 = CHECKDAYS1 + 7
input: URL
output: startSearch (search will be started)

```
IF        (days since last visit of the URL < CHECKDAYS1)
          startSearch = false
ELSEIF    (URL is valid)
          enter new date of visit;
          startSearch = false
ELSEIF    (days since last visit of the URL > CHECKDAYS2)
          startSearch = true
ELSE      startSearch = false
```

It is important to notice that the above algorithms and the determination of characteristics work completely automated.

Architecture

The architecture of HPSearch is shown in figure 3. The core of HPSearch is connected with all components. The arrows depict the data-flow. HPSearch asks queries to search engines which return result pages. Candidate Home Pages are read from the Web.

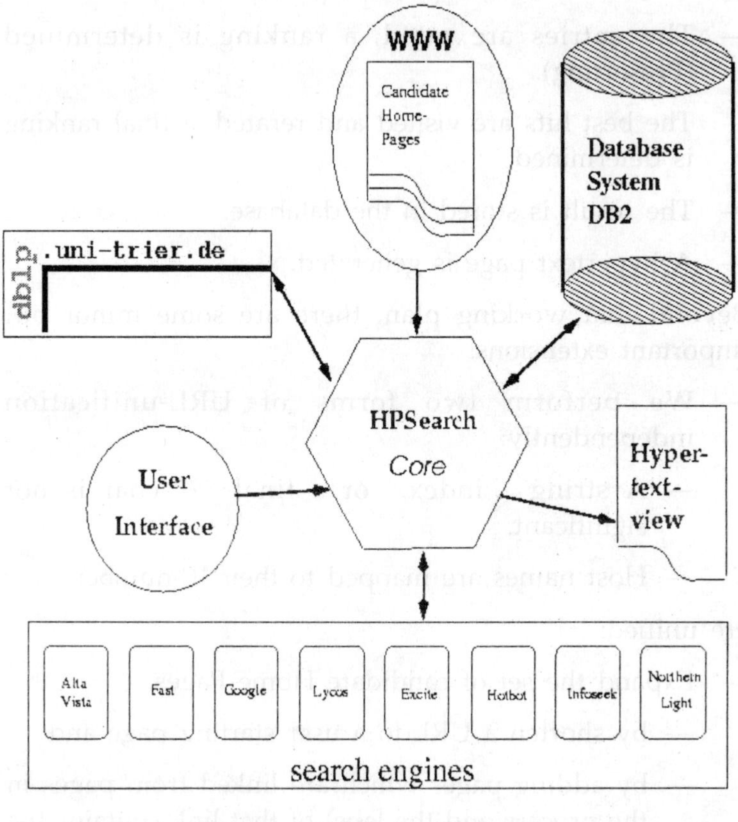

Figure 3. Architecture of HPSearch

Results are stored persistently in the database which runs with DB2. A hypertext view is generated to show the results. An export-file for DBLP is generated. With the user-interface HPSearch can be queried.

Working Plan of the Search

The search is started by a user or by the mechanisms.

— The name is ascertained.

— Queries for different search engines are generated.

— Responded pages are parsed, entries are extracted.

— The entries are rated, a ranking is determined (Presorting).

— The best hits are visited and rerated, a final ranking is determined.

— The result is stored in the database.

— A hypertext page is generated.

Beyond that working plan, there are some minor but important extensions:

— We perform two forms of URL-unification independently:

  — A string " index." or a final "/"-char is not significant.

  — Host names are mapped to their IP-number.

are unified:

— Expand the set of candidate Home Pages,

  — by shorten a URL to a user starting page and

  — by adding pages which are linked from pages in the process and the label of that link contains the name of the searched person.

HPSearch provides about 38,000 names for which a probably good Home Page was found. In an evaluation test, HPSearch searches for persons whose Home Page was entered manually in the DBLP. HPSearch found in 84 % of them a correct personal Home Page. In DBLP, only 79 % of manually entered URLs are correct, other URLs were broken or out of date . The best search engine shows the correct personal Home Page in 60 % on position 1. Some users want to send correct or remove wrong personal Home Pages. We have build a form for entering that pages. The manually entered Home Pages from DBLP are included in the HPSearch database, after URL checking.

Mops

Mops is a relatively simple search engine. Its goal is to provide an index of scientific papers found on or close to a given list of web addresses. From these documents, an index is created. It can be searched through a web interface. It answers questions by giving links to the documents containing the search items, their initial lines, and the choice to browse their contents in ASCII format.

Finding and Sorting Documents

The start point of Mops is a list of web addresses. Given a web address, it starts a search from the given address following the links down to a given depth. It turned out to be sufficient to set the depth to 1 or 2. Therefore, only a small area around each given web address is searched, what makes the search quite fast. Mops collects all postscript, dvi and pdf documents (also in compressed form) found, because scientific papers in computer science are available mostly in these formats.

For each document, the date when it was found, the sequence of links which led to it, and the "name" of the link - i.e. the text <a href=URL> name of the link </a> used by the web page's author for the description of the link - is stored. When a document was found already earlier, it is not collected again, if its last collection date is not too long ago. Anyway, its sequence of links and name is updated accordingly.

Dependent on the web address of the document, it is decided whether it is included into the collection of scientific documents, or into the collection of documents which have to do with lectures, classes, or other, non-scientific matters. Moreover, there are documents which appear under different addresses, e.g. because the web server is accessible with different names, or because a scientist belongs to different research institutes. It is tried to find these "duplicates" and to prevent that they appear more than once in the index.

Creating Index

Each document is stored in ASCII format, which is generated using pstotext This allows to use glimpseindex for creation of an index for each collection. Search through this index is available by a web interface which uses glimpse. Besides searching for documents in which certain terms appear, it is also possible to search directly for links, or to search through the names of the documents. For each document found, its original URL, its description, its initial lines and the first matching lines are shown. It is possible, to browse through the complete text of each document, and to view all the lines matching the query. Each search result can be refined by further queries.

Mops consists of a bunch of Perl scripts. It runs on an ordinary PC under a Linux operating system, and it uses lots of freely available software like glimpse, perl, pstotext, cgiwrap, apache. The search engine usually runs for 30 hours during the weekend. Afterwards, the index is updated. Here produced a CD-ROM which contains all the data used for the index search of Mops and the scripts for the Web interface. To install the Web interface on a standard Linux PC takes copying one file from the CD-ROM to the disk. One is then able to search the complete index from CD-ROM without Internet connection.

HPSearch Joins Mops

The quality of the Mops index depends on the list of starting points for the search. Mops searches only a small area around each starting point. If the starting points are too far away from the documents, they either will not be found, or the search takes too much time. Usually, scientists provide links to their scientific papers either on their Home Page or on a neighboured web page. Therefore, Home Pages are good starting points for the search.

The first Mops index was created for scientific papers in complexity theory. A "hand written" list of about 60 web addresses and a list automatically created using the interface to DBLP and HPSearch is used as starting points for the search. This list consists of Home Pages of complexity theorists, and of technical report servers of several universities. Currently, there are about 7,000 documents in the collection. On average, there are 40 new documents found each week.

Another index was created for scientific papers in the BDD area. The first step was to get the names of the scientists in this field. This was managed by querying the DBLP server for publications which have "BDD" or "Binary Decision Diagram" in its titles. The bibliographic data obtained in this way yields names of scientists of the considered field. With these names, HPSearch produced a list of personal Home Pages.

This is used as starting points for the search of Mops. Within two runs of the search engine, about 1000 scientific papers and about 250 other papers were collected. Meanwhile, few "hand written" addresses were added. The index now contains 2,500 papers. Its usefulness can be seen by the fact that the BDD portal has a link to it.

3
Virtual Collections

The traditional library evolved to provide services to make its contents more accessible to its users, the effective digital library must develop a range of services to assist its users in finding, understanding, and using its contents. Moreover, in its digital form the library has the potential to not just emulate traditional libraries in the services it provides but to improve and extend them by capitalising on advantages inherent in the medium.

One important area where the digital library can extend the services it provides beyond that of the traditional library is in integrating and highlighting user contributions. With the exception of especially unique or noteworthy contributions, the traditional library is rarely eager to receive resource contributions outside of its usual channels, as the effort needed to catalogue and integrate outside contributions into a physical library is substantial. Digital libraries, on the other hand, are more often willing to receive contributions.

It has been demonstrated that a combination of minimal submission data and basic verification procedures can result in high-quality digital library contributions with low rejection rates. Such contributions enhance the value of the digital library by increasing its size and diversity and the process of cataloguing and integrating contributed resources into a digital library often requires less effort. However, the aspects that make digital libraries built from user contributions valuable-diversity of content, potential for large growth-also create potential drawbacks.

For example, search and browse facilities enable users to find resources based on features such as author, subject, and keywords, but as a digital library grows, finding specific resources of interest among the entire collection can become more difficult. At the same time, the prominence of a given contributor's contributions becomes diminished as the library grows. One way to help users find resources of interest in a digital library while ensuring that contributors receive recognition is to borrow a concept that has long been part of traditional libraries: the special collection.

By defining and making available virtual collections we believe the digital library can extend the special collection model and-at a modest cost-provide benefits to both its users and contributors that will encourage its own growth and viability.

Traditional libraries often contain, in addition to their main holdings, special collections. In these settings a special collection is generally defined as a group of related materials that is given some form of special treatment. The special treatment might be due to the rare or delicate nature of the materials (rare books or antique maps, for example), or because the library wants to highlight the materials in some way. In contrast to traditional libraries, the special or sub-collections of digital libraries can be much more fluid.

Where the holdings of a traditional library are physically constrained to a single space and a single ordering, resources in a digital library can be distributed across many servers, can be owned by different organisations, and can be displayed in many different orderings and arrangements. This fluid nature makes defining collections and sub-collections in the digital environment less straightforward.

Adhering closely to the traditional library definition, one could consider a digital library collection to be all those resources that reside on a single server, or alternatively, all those that can be accessed though a given library's interface, even if they are physically distributed. However, even a broad definition of a collection in the context of digital libraries can be ambiguous. It can, for example, be influenced by the point of view of those making the definition. The people responsible for managing resources stored in separate databases might think of each as a distinct collection, while an end user with access to them all is more likely to consider them a single collection.

Defining sub-collections can be even more flexible as there are many possible factors that can suggest how sub-collections can be formed. A sub-collection can be defined by including all those resources that share a topic or other significant attribute (the collection of all butterfly images), those contributed by a specific organisation (the collection of Insect Museum resources), or those used for a specific purpose (all resources used for the online course in butterflies). These sub-collection examples are instances of collections that cannot be easily replicated in traditional libraries.

They are made possible by exploiting advantages the digital environment inherently provides: objects can exist in multiple collections, collections with the same objects grouped in different ways can co-exist, collections can be created dynamically and exist for varying amounts of time.

They become virtual collections and as such-in contrast to the traditional library-enable a digital library to provide a limitless number of sub-collections based on a wide range of features.

Creating Virtual Collections

Although it is common for traditional libraries to create and maintain special collections, many digital libraries do not attempt to provide a similar service. Most digital libraries do create the most basic of virtual collections-the result set dynamically created from a search request or category browsing-but rarely do they explicitly create and promote the sort of virtual collections described above. Doing so, however, can benefit both the users of the digital library and those who contribute resources to it.

A digital library that contains virtual collections helps its users in several ways. A new user who may be intimidated by a digital library's search interface or the number of results returned by a query might be better introduced to the digital library through the more easily explorable partitioned set of resources in a virtual collection. A directory of the virtual collections contained by a digital library, can provide a good introduction and overview of the library's contents to new or casual users.

Associating resources with virtual collections enables those resources to be found more easily, either by browsing the contents of a highlighted virtual collection or through standard search and browse interfaces. Adding virtual collections to search facilities, such as that of the iLumina digital library of educational resources, enables a user to perform a standard search but restrict it to a specific virtual collection, which could provide a more manageable and higher-quality result set than by searching the entire digital library.

Looking at the use of the digital library from a "work-oriented perspective", other benefits to the user stem from a more productive use of time. In it is suggested that sub-collections can facilitate work by isolating a group of related content and enabling a user to focus on those resources. Defining virtual collections makes it easier for users to find and work with such groupings of related content, either through a listing of available collections, or by a "related resources" link based on virtual collection associations and tied to specific resources. Additionally, the virtual collection description might include links to related information outside the digital library, thus guiding users to more materials for their work.

In most cases those who contribute resources to digital libraries (at least not-for-profit libraries, such as the new National SMETE Digital Library (NSDL)) are not directly compensated, yet digital libraries often depend largely on contributions for the content they provide. It is, therefore, in the best interests of the digital library to find ways to encourage new and repeat contributions. Virtual collections can benefit contributors in several ways. First, they provide an alternative distribution outlet. Contributors often have collections in which they have invested effort in creating and would like to see used more widely.

Because a digital library will generally have a much larger base of regular users than the contributor, contributing the collection gives the contributor's resources more exposure. By grouping a contributor's resources through a virtual collection the digital library helps maintain the resources' association with the contributor and in effect provides publicity and recognition to contributors. By explicitly highlighting virtual collections and the people and organisations that contributed them, a digital library can increase the visibility of contributors. As a result, contributors are likely to benefit from more traffic to their own web sites, and can point people to their contributions at hosting digital library.

Virtual collections can not only help improve the "brand" of a set of resources and support their distribution, but can also offer basic infrastructure services. In some cases, such as with the Open Video Project where the resources (video files) are quite large, contributing resources enables the contributor to share resources without the overhead of storing and managing them, while retaining an association with them. If a contributor owns a large number of resources, this is a significant benefit itself, and one that has been taken advantage of by several Open Video Project contributors.

Finally, if the digital library shares information about resource usage, either directly to its contributors or as is increasingly common, through most recommended or top-10 lists, the contributor can gauge the relative demand of his contributions. This is helpful not only to contributors and the users of the digital library, but also "helps new contributors understand what is considered a good item".

Implementing Virtual Collections

The benefits of virtual collections do not come without a price, of course. For a digital library to be able to easily create and remove virtual collections, to associate resources with different virtual collections in a flexible way, and to help users find and use the virtual collections, the library must have a structured approach to representing these collections. Moreover, to make creating such collections practical, this approach should also strive to minimise the costs associated with creating virtual collections.

Collection-Level Metadata

Metadata is a key element of any library, traditional or digital. Metadata is used by libraries to describe and organise item-level resources and by users to search and browse the library. Collection-level metadata performs a similar function for collections and is used in traditional libraries for discovery across collections. Work on collection-level metadata from several fields including archives, museums, libraries, and the Internet is relevant to the design and implementation of virtual collections.

As outlined in, each field defines collections differently and has different standards governing collection description. The past few years have seen a movement to create a standard for collection description that is informed by, yet transcends, the fields from which it is derived. Work in the UK and the US has resulted in the formulation of goals for collection-level metadata and the definition and development of schemas to describe collections.

Based on work with the eLib working group on Collection Level Descriptions, the RIDING Clump Project created a searchable database of collection descriptions to provide information about what was available in its libraries. The purpose of its scheme was to describe any type of collection-physical or virtual (electronic), networked or otherwise. RIDING collection metadata should allow users to discover, locate and access collections, search across multiple collections and allow software to provide services based on user preferences.

The Research Support Libraries Programme (RSLP) Collection Description Project developed a model allowing all the projects in its programme to describe collections in a consistent, machine readable way. The RSLP builds upon the RIDING goals above by requiring that collection metadata allow the refinement of distributed searching approaches based on the characteristics of collections. The Alexandria Digital Library (ADL) is a research digital library project focused on geo-referenced geo-spatial information. The goal of the ADL is to create a single model that supports the four roles ADL identified for collection metadata: collection registration, network discovery, user documentation, and management.

First, it highlights the importance of establishing standardised collectionlevel metadata schemas that can effectively describe and manage a diverse set of collections and their metadata. Second, it argues that the schemas must support a number of functional library services that enable users to access collections and items, to search for materials, and to comprehend and use them effectively.

Types of Metadata

One challenge to creating collection-level metadata noted in the literature is the potentially high cost of production. Metadata can be automatically-generated or human-created with the latter clearly imposing more significant costs in terms of human effort and time. In the context of collections, describes two types of roughly corresponding metadata: inherent metadata, or information that can be extracted from the resource objects themselves, such as total number of objects or total file-size of the collection; and contextual metadata, or metadata which involves human judgment to create, such as a textual description of a collection of resources.

There are significant advantages to utilising inherent metadata as much as possible. Because it can be generated automatically, inherent metadata has minimal costs associated with its creation and maintenance and can be updated on a regular, automated schedule. In contrast, human-created metadata is time-consuming, error-prone, costly to create, and more likely to be inconsistent. A person assigned to create metadata may only perform this task on an occasional, as-needed basis, and it may be a lower priority task than others for which that person is also responsible.

Inconsistencies in metadata assigned to resources can arise due to variations in a given cataloguer's judgment over time and because different cataloguers may make varied judgements in cataloguing resources. There are drawbacks to relying solely on inherent metadata to define virtual collections, however. A risk in complete automation is the loss of many of the benefits of creating a virtual collection. Contextual metadata is important because it enables us to give some character and cohesiveness to the virtual collection. Indeed, a collection.

The use of contextual metadata and human judgment in selecting resources to be included in a virtual collection has other benefits. Virtual collections can be described "in terms of expected use in addition to being characterised by the terms they actually contain". Resources can be more carefully chosen for inclusion in a virtual collection, with consideration of expected use, resulting in a more concise collection of high-quality resources that is easier to for the user to search or browse.

It is important to recognise, however, that a collection-level schema that relies heavily on contextual metadata is relatively costly to implement and thus less likely to be maintained in the long term. A more viable approach is to define a schema for virtual collections that balances the costs and benefits of each type of metadata. In short, a cost-effective schema should include useful inherent metadata, supplemented by contextual metadata that captures human judgments of a collection's nature and the selection of criteria for inclusion in the collection.

Virtual Collections in iLumina and Open Video

To ensure the schema was sufficiently general, we applied it to two very different digital libraries: iLumina, a library of sharable undergraduate teaching materials for science, mathematics, technology, and engineering; and Open Video, a shared digital video repository and test collection. Each digital library contains more than 1000 items and accepts contributions from anyone, subject to review before being made publicly available. Substantial collections of resources have been contributed to each digital library by a single person or organisation.

In iLumina's case, these collections include a group of light and electron microscope images (micrographs), several hundred "physlets," or small physics applets, and a collection of images and related information of butterfly and moth caterpillars. In the Open Video digital library, substantial contributions of video footage have come from a handful of organisations, including the Internet Archive, Carnegie Mellon's Informedia Project, and the University of Maryland's Human Computer Interaction Laboratory. A unique aspect of the Open Video Project is the large size of its video files, which has encouraged contributions from some organisations that lack the resources to store their video themselves.

In both iLumina and Open Video the resources of their subcollections can be found through various searching and browsing mechanisms. However, for reasons discussed earlier, we felt that creating virtual collections to represent the contributed sub-collections would benefit both the contributors and the users of these digital libraries. Specifically, our primary motivations for developing virtual collections were similar in each case: to highlight the work of authors/creators who contributed a critical mass of materials on a topic, to streamline the creation of itemlevel metadata, and to provide users with another way of accessing and understanding the items available.

Defining a Collection-Level Schema

RSLP's collection description schema was chosen by iLumina and Open Video because the set of elements was universal, yet provided the flexibility for customisation, if needed. The RSLP schema was also selected because it is based on the Dublin Core schema. Dublin Core is a common item-level schema used by many digital libraries, which would facilitate mapping elements and exchanging data. Previous work from the RSLP and the Collection Description Focus resulted in thorough documentation, which facilitated understanding and implementing the schema in a relatively short amount of time.

Other projects currently use the RSLP schema to describe large, unrelated, relatively static physical collections in a digital environment. Our unique contribution is to use the RSLP schema to describe "born digital" objects of varying granularities, with varying relationships and at varying stages of collection growth in a digital library. However, the fact that RSLP is typically applied to physical collections meant that some elements and cataloguing notes were not relevant to describing collections in a digital environment.

This did not minimise the universal nature of the element set or render the schema unusable, but it did require us to review all the RSLP elements and choose the ones most appropriate to digital collections. iLumina and Open Video formulated requirements used to select RSLP elements, and, more generally, to measure the success of implementing the RSLP schema. These included:

— Identifying a subset of useful elements that would yield informative and easily understood collection descriptions

— Minimising the cost, in time and resources, of creating collection-level metadata

Useful collection descriptions can be created by identifying a subset of elements relevant to users, by ensuring that metadata is complete within a collection description and consistent across collections and by presenting descriptions in an easily understood interface. Low-cost metadata creation can be accomplished by harvesting metadata automatically, by requiring the collection creator, rather than a cataloguer, to describe their collections and by providing an efficient cataloguing tool.

Using the complete RSLP schema, collection-level descriptions were created for iLumina, Open Video and their sub-collections. It was important to identify the metadata source (item-level record, collection creator, subject-area reviewer) to track the cost of creating metadata. By starting with the complete schema we identified elements that aided understanding the collection. This process also identified extraneous elements, which were not included in the collection record interface and the collection cataloguing tool being developed. The resulting subset of elements met our requirements: collection descriptions could be created with minimal cost while providing sufficient information to aid discovery.

Implementation of the Collection-Level Schema

The subset of elements used to catalogue collections in iLumina and Open Video; the RSLP suggested use for each field; and, the iLumina and Open Video decisions about the type of data to include in each field and who provides the information. The RSLP schema contains 46 elements.

Originally, iLumina and Open Video implemented a subset of eleven. After another iteration of testing and design, iLumina has implemented sixteen and Open Video seventeen RSLP elements.

The element subset records four types of information about collections: a description, access policies, relationships to other collections, and collection owner contact information. The subset was chosen because the initial cataloguing process consistently yielded data for these elements. The subset also matched the types of data reflected in item-level records. This provided users with consistent information between item and collection.

During the initial implementation, four listed elements were not included in the subset: Type and the three elements related to time. Because the RSLP schema has been used to describe physical collections, the developers created a controlled vocabulary to distinguish between collection types. We used the type element during the initial cataloguing process, but found that the collections in iLumina and Open Video were often of the same type, so the same vocabulary terms were used repeatedly with no distinction. Also, the terms would have to be explained to collection contributors and users, which could be a barrier to cataloguing, using, and comprehending the collections.

Recently, however, Open Video incorporated the type element into its schema as a means to distinguish between virtual collections created for different purposes, such as collections organised around a specific contributor and collections containing resources from different contributors intended for a special purpose, such as a test collection. Rather than using the RSLP controlled vocabulary for Type, which classifies collections by curatorial environment, content or policy, Open Video created a new vocabulary more appropriate to its online resources.

iLumina has not yet incorporated the type element but the new vocabulary Open Video has implemented for Type may be integrated into iLumina in the future. Initially, iLumina and Open Video did not implement the three time elements because they seemed more applicable to physical collections. However, informal feedback indicated that users preferred to see metadata about time because it aided understanding the collection. As a result, iLumina and Open Video included two elements.

After identifying a useful subset of elements that would inspire our schema, we next considered how to minimise the cost of determining values for those elements and how to extend the possibilities for expressing relationships between collections. The cost of creating collection-level metadata can be reduced by automatically populating fields in the collection description. In iLumina and Open Video, "manually-entered" metadata is provided by the collection creator via a cataloguing tool or by a subject-area reviewer when the collection-level metadata is examined.

"Automatically populated" metadata is derived from querying specific fields of item-level resources within the collection. The Alexandria Digital Library uses "automatic" to describe the process of harvesting inherent metadata from the resources themselves and not from item-level descriptions. In the case of iLumina and Open Video, collection descriptions are completely comprised of contextual metadata that is manually entered either at the item or collection level. Currently three fields in the subset can be automatically populated with metadata from the item-level description.

For collection description to be cost-effective, the cost of item-level metadata creation must be minimised and more fields in the collection description must be automatically populated. Implementing a cataloguing tool with a usable interface for collection contributors is another way to reduce the cost of creating collection-level metadata. In the prototyped collection cataloguing tool, metadata for other fields will be supplied in drop-down menus with standardised vocabulary or text boxes that can be modified by collection contributors or reviewers.

This will ensure consistency in collection description. Also, a well-designed interface with clear instructions should minimise the cost of metadata creation in terms of a contributor's time. For example, when a collection record is rendered in XML, the elements retain their RSLP attributes; however, field names were changed on the interface (RSLP attribute "Concept" becomes "Keyword"; "Super Collection" becomes "Collection is Part Of").

iLumina and Open Video hope to pass the majority of the cataloguing costs on to its collection contributors as a trade-off for having the collection publicised. iLumina will incur some cost through the involvement of the subject-area reviewer as they error-check metadata and recommend changes. One aspect of metadata creation that iLumina contributors and subject-area reviewers share is identifying the relationships between collections and expressing them through the relational fields.

These relationships can be applied to collections of varying sizes and granularity, which shows the relational fields for the iLumina Digital Library, which shows the Physlets virtual collection within iLumina. Though relationships are currently noted manually, in the future, relationships between collections could be inferred automatically. For example, when the Physlet record notes in field "Collection is Part Of" that it is contained in iLumina, then the iLumina record would automatically reflect the Physlet collection in the field Contains Sub-collections.

As collection-level metadata becomes widely used, we believe the relational attributes will be essential not only for discovering resources within single repositories, but also across digital libraries, such as the National SMETE Digital Library (NSDL). As it is currently envisioned, the NSDL will be a highly distributed set of collections and sub-collections tied together by a core integration system that coordinates services on the collections for users across the country.

However, the larger and more distributed the NSDL becomes, the more difficult it will be for users to find valuable resources and the (often small) collections they need. By explicitly representing not only a wealth of virtual collections, but also the relationships among them, regardless of their physical location, a collection-level metadata schema should greatly improve the navigability of the NSDL.

4

Digital Library Components

Comprehensive digital libraries will help users manage all phases of the information lifecycle. This is illustrated in Figure 1, which summarises much of the discussion of a US National Science Foundation funded workshop on Social Aspects of Digital Libraries. Of particular import is to simplify the authoring and creation processes so that wider populations can participate, adding all types of multimedia content directly into digital libraries.

Downstream access allows readers to benefit from this type of computer-mediated communication, across time and space. Ultimately, it is hoped that knowledge will be shared and then lead to additional cycles of discovery, authoring, and utilisation that are facilitated by digital libraries. Digital libraries are distinguished in that they afford services connected with each of the phases of the lifecycle. They integrate technologies from a variety of disciplines to help realise the designs articulated by early visionaries.

Vannevar Bush was one of the first to clearly describe problems related to the modern explosion of information and to appeal to technology to help us meet our needs regarding scholarly communication. Twenty years later,

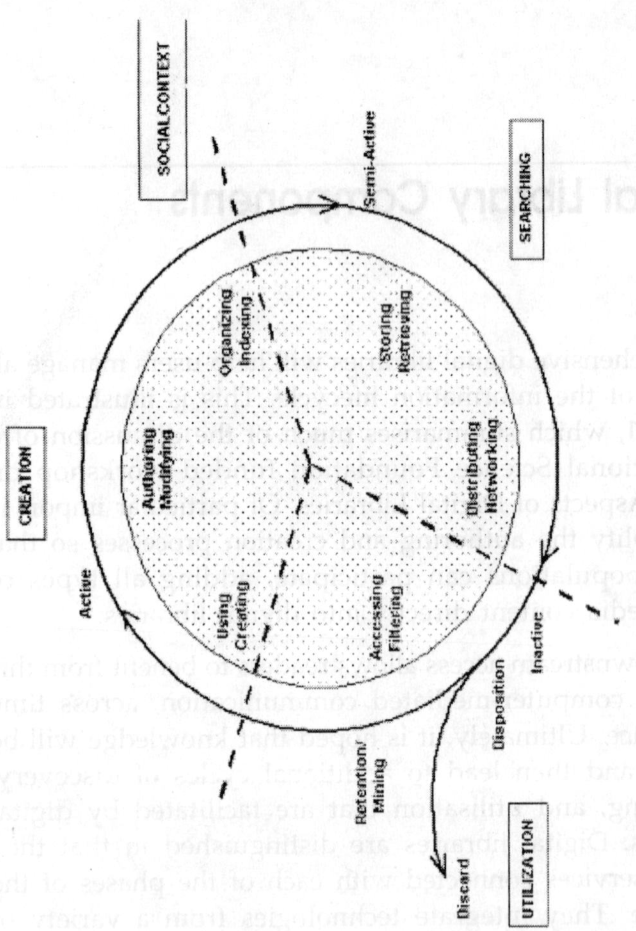

Figure 1. Information Life Cycle

Licklider painted a more complete picture, identifying the needs for better distributed-processing, human-computer interaction, document management, and retrieval. Salton helped launch the modern era of automatic indexing and search through some 30 years of laboratory research. But real development of digital libraries per se only began in the early 1990s, drawing upon such visions, as well as statements of needs and requirements from prospective users.

Work on early projects like TULIP, ongoing efforts to reach consensus and establish standards like the Dublin Core Metadata Initiative, and several rounds of research funding, have all helped lay a firm foundation as a clearer understanding of the scope of the field has emerged.

Digital libraries are complex systems that:

1. help satisfy information needs of users (societies),
2. provide information services (scenarios),
3. locate and present information in usable ways (spaces),
4. organise information in usable ways (structures), and
5. communicate information with users and computers (streams).

To build digital libraries we must ensure that each of the "S" constructs is addressed, and so can use 5S as a checklist or guideline. In operational terms, however, many digital libraries are built out of components that are integrated into a production quality system.

Digital Objects

The actual content of digital libraries is made up of a number of digital objects. In some cases these may be thought of as data sets (e.g., a table of results, the genomic information for an individual). In others they may be multimedia information, such as an image, graphic, animation, sound, musical performance, or video. Many can be thought of as documents, which carry content in some structure or structures, perhaps made up of logical or physical divisions such as sections or pages.

Thus, into the foreseeable future, digital libraries will be hybrid constructs, where paper, microforms, and other media carry much of the content that is of interest and only the metadata is in digital form.

METADATA

Digital objects are described, structured, summarised, managed, and otherwise manipulated in surrogate form through the use of "metadata", which literally means data about data. Three types of metadata are often distinguished: descriptive, structural, and administrative. Metadata is usually produced through a process called "cataloguing" that is often carried out by trained librarians. Collections of such information are commonly stored in "catalogues". In computerised environments, metadata may be automatically or semi-automatically extracted or derived from the original content, or the "full-text" may simply be indexed and searched without involving metadata.

Nevertheless, if metadata is available and can be used along with content terms derived from full-text documents, the result is better than if only one source of evidence is employed. Yet, if only metadata is available in computer form to describe a digital object, it must be used in digital libraries. Hence, metadata should be used whenever available in a digital library, and is an important aspect in many such systems.

Repositories

As can be seen in Figure 2, we can think of digital libraries as containing a collection of digital objects (DOs), each of which has one or more sets of metadata objects (MDOs) associated. This "repository" part of a digital library may, as is the case in the Open Archives Initiative, follow certain conventions. In particular, according to the latest specifications, an "Open Archive" (OA) is a computer system with a WWW server that behaves according to an OA protocol to allow other computers to harvest metadata from it. That protocol supports requests to, for example:

— list what types of metadata format are present,

— list what structure of sets and subsets are used to organise or partition the content,

— disseminate or return a particular MDO, or

— list URIs (unique identifiers) for all MDOs added during a particular date range.

In particular, every OA must be able to return MDOs that conform to the Dublin Core and are coded in XML. They must have documented policies about what DOs are included, what "archiving" is in place, and what terms and conditions apply to use, if any. Having a repository component that is an OA means that access to digital library content is open, ensuring widespread interoperability at one important level. At a slightly deeper level, interoperability among digital libraries requires that digital objects be accessible through some scheme for universal identifier names (e.g., URNs).

MDOs thus have an URN that facilitates access (if authorised) to the corresponding DO. A likely policy for an OA is to use some specific type of URN (e.g., OCLC's PURL or CNRI's handle—also employed for Digital Object

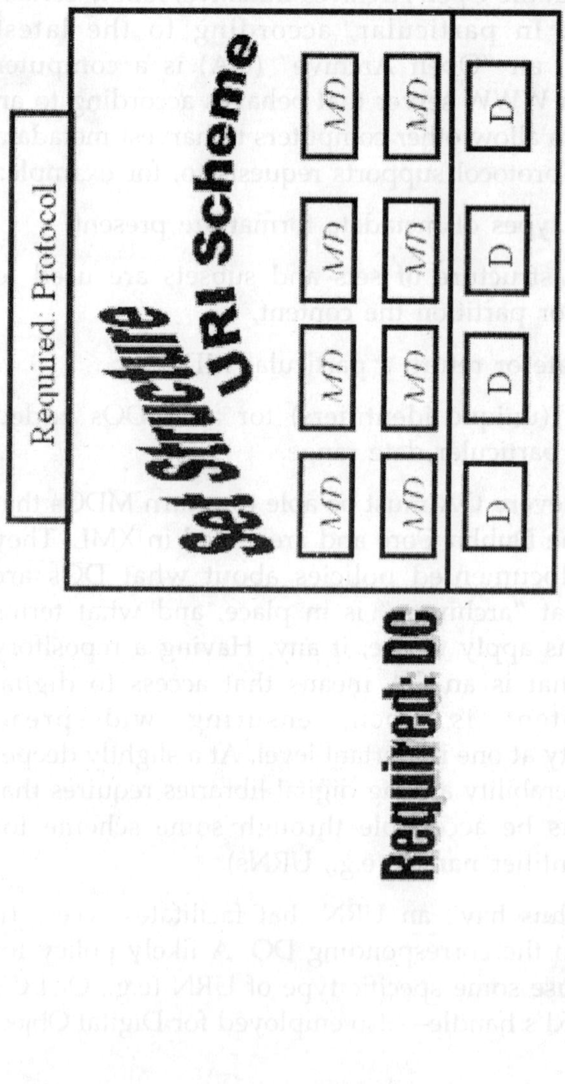

Figure 2. Open Archives Repository

Identifiers, DOIs). In today's ubiquitous WWW environment, it is presumed that users and computers will be able to retrieve a desired DO if its identifier is known.

Management of Rights

In the trivial case, which fortunately is common, content is freely available so nothing is needed here. In some cases too, where content is encrypted, content management is outside the scope of the digital library, since secure objects are stored and retrieved and the steps of encryption and decryption occur remotely. Similarly, some content may have "watermarks" added in a way that makes removal difficult, so that subsequent access outside the digital library can be monitored or controlled.

However, as e-commerce, e-government, and other movements spread, it will be crucial for many digital libraries to manage rights. This typically involves a number of steps:

1. The digital library should include policies and rules specifying the management required.
2. The users of the digital library should be authenticated in some way so they are known.
3. The content of the digital library should be shown to be authentic.
4. Payment should be made if access requires that in a particular case.
5. Users who are authorised to access a DO are allowed to do so.
6. Subsequent access with the DO may take place after retrieval to a user's site.

IBM has developed sophisticated technology and digital

library systems with support for rights management. Xerox staff has developed a Digital Property Rights Language that relates to step 1 above. Password schemes and systems like Kerberos relate to step 2. Hashing with MD5 or use of digital signatures can support step 3. E-commerce mechanisms, especially those enabling micro-payments or subscriptions, relate to step 4. Rules processing relates to step 5, as was done at Case Western Reserve University - employing Prologue to work with users, user classes, documents, and document classes - in order to find the lowest cost access solution. In step 6, there usually is little control, unless a scheme like IBM's Cryptolope mechanism is involved wherein the DO is encapsulated with code that limits access (e.g., prohibits printing).

Indexing, Resource Discovery, Searching, and Retrieving

DOs and/or MDOs are automatically indexed so that some index structure is built to speed up search. Such indexing may build upon any manual indexing carried out by authors, other creators, or indexers. Automatic indexing also may involve first classifying DOs, such as when OCLC's CORC project software suggests Dewey Decimal Classification entries for a WWW page that is being catalogued.

Indexes may be centralised or distributed. They may be two-level, allowing a resource discovery phase to proceed to find what source(s) should be included in the subsequent (lower) level search. Indexes also may have multiple parts, such as when a document has text, image, audio, or video content. Content-based indexing of multimedia information generally involves identifying and assessing features that characterise the DOs, whether they involve concepts, n-grams, words, keywords, descriptors, phonemes, textures, colour histograms, eigenvalues, links, or user ratings.

Most commonly, searching in a digital library involves an information retrieval system or search engine. In some cases a database management system is used instead or underlies the retrieval system. In any case, retrieval will be more effective if a suitable scheme is used to combine the various types of evidence available, to indicate if a DO may be relevant with respect to the query that is used to express the user's information need.

Linking, Annotating, and Browsing

Once a DO is found, it often is appropriate to follow links from it to cited works (or vice versa). Further, notes can be recorded as annotations and linked back to the works, so they can be recalled later or shared with colleagues as part of collaborative activities. If suitable clustering is in place, other DOs that are "near" a given work may be examined. Or, using a classification system appropriate for the content domain, users may browse around in "concept space" and link at any point between concepts and related DOs. Browsing also can proceed based on any of the elements in the MDO. Thus, dates, locations, publishers, contributing artists, language, and other aspects may be considered to explore the collection or refine a search.

Interaction and Interfaces

Ultimately, users will connect through a human-computer interface and interact with the digital library, though in some cases the digital library may be an embedded system that is seen only indirectly (e.g., through a word processor that allows one to search for a quotation). Most commonly, a digital library has an interface for users to search, browse, follow links, retrieve, and read documents.

For example, the Computer Science Teaching Centre, a digital library of courseware about computing, requests that all users, except those just browsing or searching, login to identify themselves. Then it knows and tailors the interface so that suitably authorised users can submit, review, or edit works. Further, CSTC encourages users to submit courseware they have developed that others might download, and supports their entering in suitable metadata as well as uploading their applets, demonstrations, laboratory exercises, interactive multimedia training resources, etc.

After the work has been entered by the creator, it can be improved through peer review and "certified" for public use, or even accepted for publication in the ACM Journal of Educational Resources in Computing (JERIC). Thus, instead of requiring current complex and expensive chains of processing for journal submissions, handling with digital libraries may be implemented through this "users direct" model. Following retrieval, users examine a list of results or else work with more sophisticated schemes for visualising and managing results. Many other types of rich interaction are possible through innovative digital library interfaces.

In particular digital libraries may use special software to present or render multimedia, hypertext, and hypermedia content. Such software may be launched from a WWW browser, which typically only supports a limited range of hypermedia. Real-time requirements must be satisfied to ensure adequate quality of service when streaming content is involved, especially if multiple streams are involved.

Also related to interaction with the digital library is the matter of workflow management. Especially with the "users direct" model, the various people interacting with a particular DO may leave some record of approval or review, which triggers others to continue with processing. For example, universities that are part of the Networked Digital Library of Theses and Dissertations allow students to upload their works, make changes, secure approval by the graduate school, have cataloguing information added by librarians, and ultimately release the suitably enhanced information for widespread access.

Many digital libraries will have their own user interfaces. In addition, they may support gateway connections, using protocols like Dienst or Z39.50 (International Standard Maintenance Agency Z39.50, 2000). As we work toward world digital libraries, we must ensure that our interfaces support multimedia and multilingual access, as well as various schemes for interconnection with other digital libraries and resources.

Since the field of digital libraries is young, there still is active investigation regarding architecture, interconnection, and interoperability. Given the range of legacy systems that are used today as parts of digital libraries, the actual situation often is more complex. To simplify matters, several interconnection strategies have been explored. At Stanford, a bus approach has been used. Mediation code "wraps" around various collections or resources to make suitable conversions to representations supported by the bus and the other services connected to it.

Agents provide another interconnection mechanism. Many agent-based systems use KQML as the language for transporting knowledge constructs. Yet another approach is the distributed scheme supporting federated search that underlies the Dienst system. Nevertheless, currently it is not possible to identify the best architecture(s) for digital libraries. We must look to future technological developments and actual deployments as well as standardised performance testing to resolve such questions.

Since the early 1990s, the digital library field has emerged as an important area of research and development. There are hundreds of projects and thousands of reports/publications describing them. One of the active research programmes is in the USA, funded by the National Science Foundation. A summary of that Digital Libraries Initiative makes clear the broad scope of work underway. NSF has deliberately selected a diverse set of content areas, genre, media, and user communities in an effort to rapidly develop the field.

Work on digital libraries has been facilitated by technical advances in many areas. For the first time, storage systems are readily affordable that can handle enormous text collections, very large image collections, and large audio or video collections. Fast processors, supercomputers, cluster-computers, networks of workstations, and other computational aids have provided ample processing capacity to handle user communities operating on a global scale. Increases in network speeds and bandwidth have made it possible to build distributed systems that perform well and have high reliability.

Computationally expensive algorithms have been refined so that useful techniques such as LSI can help with multilingual retrieval and other applications. High-end graphics systems and virtual environments also have evolved to be usable for information visualisation as well as interfacing with digital libraries. Representation schemes like PDF and XML have made digital documents easy to produce and share; facilitating information interchange and encouraging further digitisation. An example of the effects of technology can be seen with regard to the

MARIAN digital library system developed at Virginia Tech.

Over the last decade, coding has switched from C to C++ to Java. Hardware has switched from mainframes to minis to PCs. Current work to enhance performance includes development of new algorithms to manipulate inverted files on the Virginia Tech PetaPlex system, which has 100 processors and 2.5 terabytes of disk storage capacity. Earlier studies of performance demonstrated that the architecture is scalable, and showed that, for example, changing some of the internal communication from TCP to UDP would lead to substantive improvement.

Related Issues

According to the 5S framework, the topmost level deals with "societies". Though technology has made possible many advances in digital libraries, all such efforts are situated in a social context, as can be seen in Figure 1. Many of the key social issues were identified in a NSF-funded workshop on this topic. Underlying work on the Networked Digital Library of Theses and Dissertations is a strong social and educational rationale, to prepare the next generation of scholars for the Information Age.

Its aims - of encouraging discussion about intellectual property rights among students and faculty, of building awareness and infrastructure about digital libraries on campuses, and of developing a new genre for communication among graduate students and researchers - are largely being met. The impact of economics is remarkable, in that making works available for free leads to hundreds or thousands of downloads per work per year. This contrasts with interlibrary loan or buying copies for roughly $50, which very rarely led to more than 5 accesses per year.

Social and technical issues often relate. For example, the culture and social atmosphere determines how electronic theses and dissertations will be managed on a particular campus, or across broader boundaries involving states or nations. Universities with advanced infrastructure, like Caltech, MIT, and Virginia Tech, have their own services. On the other hand, there are regional/national projects associated with NDLTD in Ohio, Catalunya, Australia, Germany, India, Portugal, and South Africa. Because of this arrangement, a federated search mechanism was implemented, though future plans call for use of Open Archives and regular harvesting. Groups that own content or have a tradition of managing it can continue to do so, while at the same time technical approaches can allow comprehensive search across such distributed collections.

Legal issues also become more visible with digital libraries. There often was little concern over copyright issues when preparing a dissertation that would largely go unread, sitting on a shelf in a local library. However, with the potential of thousands of downloads from around the world, authors must be very careful not to include a copyrighted image or other content without permission. Other economic, social, and legal issues have come to the fore with digital libraries.

In many states, like Virginia, a single university library can run a service for the whole state, further extending the benefits of volume purchasing. On the other hand, many such services involve a contract with an information provider that often has a complex set of terms and conditions, meaning that libraries now require more legal counsel.

Digital libraries allow new groups to assemble around new collections of interest. In many countries, digital libraries show promise regarding preserving cultural, historic, and linguistic records. In a number of situations, they have the potential of aiding economic development by supporting localised and distance education.

There are hundreds of digital library efforts underway around the world. A good place to find out about many of these is in D-Lib Magazine, which by the end of 2000 has about 1000 entries. The National Science Foundation in USA has funded the Digital Libraries Initiative, with awards granted in 1994, 1998, and 1999. Well over $50M has gone to a wide range of research projects. NSF support to Stanford University through this programme has led in part to the appearance of Google, one of the most popular search services on WWW.

Other technical advances have led to methods for processing and searching collections of images, music, and video. A great expansion in work on geographic information systems and other spatial data has also resulted. Microsoft's TerraServer demonstrates how very large data collections can serve huge user communities in spite of using relatively modest hardware resources. The museum community has demonstrated methods of accessing distributed cultural heritage information.

Sacred and/or precious resources, including antiquities, have become available from sources such as the Vatican. Special collections, such as of butterflies or floristic information, have become accessible through digital libraries. In some ways the broadest and most influential digital library efforts have to do with education. For example, in USA, after years of study, it was decided that NSF should support development of a digital library to support learning by students. This has led to over $50M committed to the National Science (and Mathematics, Engineering, and Technology Education) Digital Library, which should be launched by the end of 2002. Many thousands of teachers, and millions of students, will benefit from this resource as it aims to enhance learning through dynamic interaction, visualisation, simulation, and other computer-related devices.

5

Creation of Instructional Materials

Information technology provides not one or two, but several ways of improving the development of instruction and learning materials. Some options are relatively simple extensions of current methods, while others are novel. Information technology not only provides new options for instruction delivery, it can also help create new instruction and learning materials. In turn, these new methods and tools can address some of the key challenges for higher education, including responding more nimbly to changes in demand and competing with new providers.

Traditional Methods of Production

To simplify slightly, the traditional pipeline for producing educational materials has four key components:

— Authors create documents.

— Publishers mainly manufacture and market copies of these products.

— Libraries primarily acquire, store, and distribute copies of the products to the nearby community.

— Readers consume the products.

These groups have played relatively stable roles in the publication process for decades, even centuries. However, information technology is changing these roles; equally important, it is transforming the copyright and intellectual-property-rights laws that underpin relationships among the participants.

The simplest view of this change argues that new information technologies will reduce, perhaps even eliminate, the need for publishers and libraries. Historically, publishers and libraries have been essential intermediaries, enabling authors and audiences to reach one another. Authors rarely possessed the tools, skills, and capital necessary to typeset their books, calculate the size of production runs, or coordinate with vendors.

By the same token, individual readers (especially students and researchers) rarely could afford to acquire vast libraries of literary holdings. Publishers and libraries have traditionally met these needs. However, as educational products become increasingly digital and networked, one line of argument goes, the latter two groups may prove unnecessary, at least from a technical perspective. Today, academic research provides the most-impressive examples of how higher education is exploiting information technology to simplify the document-production pipeline.

Although individual publishers have been quick to add organisation and decoration, many of these works, in their simplest form, comprise a collection of homepages that can be read at a distance using any Web browser. Provided that you know the Internet location of an online journal, accessing the current issue is simply a matter of entering the address and reading what comes up on your screen. This kind of publication is gaining popularity for several reasons.

Cutting out the traditional publisher intermediary not only dramatically speeds up the rate at which new ideas get into "print"; it also cuts publication costs and provides a direct link to readers, who can access the papers from anywhere on the Internet as soon as they are available. The audience, in turn, is often encouraged to be publishers in return, using e-mail to send feedback and reviews on articles directly back to authors.

Finally, problems of calibrating production runs, disposing of unsold inventory, and dealing with unsatisfied consumer demand simply do not arise with digital, networked publications. No longer do students and faculty need to wait for other scholars to return copies of popular books: They simply print their own copies on demand.

Digital Libraries

If libraries existed only to store copies of books and other physical artifacts, and to share them with members of nearby communities, then the preceding examples might suggest that such institutions are in danger of extinction. Not surprisingly, traditional libraries are not ready to give up the ghost just yet. Along with publishers, whose traditional roles are similarly threatened, libraries are attempting to redefine their functions in ways that maintain roles for them in the delivery of information in digital, networked environments.

New digital libraries can try to go beyond being paperless versions of traditional libraries in at least three ways. First, freed of the need to store copies of (sometimes rare) documents, they can focus more on services that will help students and faculty find and organise information in vast virtual collections. Second, freed of the need to maintain collections in locations physically near their communities of readers, they can plan to aggregate virtual holdings into more encompassing, complete, and up-to-date collections.

And, third, freed of the dominance of static print (audio and video can be digitised as readily as can typed text), digital libraries can grapple with the complexities of representing and cataloguing new multimedia documents. A number of projects are engaged in the important, but painfully slow, translation of paper products into digital form. Project Gutenberg, for example, aims to have 10,000 texts online by the year 2001; with a growing network of volunteers, it is now downloading about eight new titles per month.

The project's mission is to provide universal access to texts. For this reason, it is digitising only materials in the public domain, and it is using the most basic storage format: "plain vanilla ASCII." Already today, then, a student using almost any computer coupled to the Internet can read the complete works of Shakespeare.

The National Digital Library, part of the Library of Congress, has used its considerable resources to digitise several hundred thousand Library holdings. Not limited to simple text, these holdings range from documents of the Continental Congress, to turn-of-the-century films, to Matthew Brady's Civil War photographs. Many students and scholars are even now making serious use of the Library's historical collections, reference materials, and search tools.

As impressive as these conversion efforts are, though, even a quick scan of the burgeoning literature on digital libraries shows that most of the action is elsewhere. Few of the universities funded through the Digital Libraries Initiative, for instance, have yet to build or acquire substantial digital holdings. Rather, they are developing tools and software agents with which digital libraries can be constructed and can be effectively searched by students, faculty, and researchers.

To anyone who has browsed the WWW-which itself can be viewed as a vast and unorganised digital library-the need for these search and management tools is obvious. Most of the information available on the Internet today is of questionable quality, at best. As holdings merge, it will become more and more difficult to find high-quality products, let alone products relevant to a chosen topic. Even more problematic, traditional tools for managing this search probably will not help much in new digital libraries.

Quite aside from the fact that traditional schemes barely work even today (card catalogs and huge cross-referencing tomes almost always seem to need the skills of experienced librarians), these print-indexing tools simply do not scale up well to multimedia documents that include several varieties of visual and auditory materials, as well as text. The hope is that a new generation of digital library tools and software agents will be able to understand multimedia documents, and that they will be as easy to use as they are powerful.

Some of these tools are little more than user-friendly search engines, which find titles through keyword searches. But others might fulfill, in electronic form, many of the roles of a personalised library assistant or online note-taker.

Single Libraries into Mega-Libraries

Another way in which libraries are trying to grow beyond their paper counterparts is simply to merge holdings. Such aggregation rarely happens in traditional libraries: One-of-a-kind documents are closely guarded and are regarded as highly limited resources that curators are naturally reluctant to part with; the cost of moving, recataloguing, and repositioning artifacts usually is prohibitive; and merging libraries into a centralised location threatens to reduce access to materials by many readers in the affected communities.

Access to materials in digital libraries, by contrast, is independent of distance, so merging can only add to the resources available to communities. Moreover, merging digital holdings is comparatively trivial. Sometimes, libraries can be merged just by adding a few well-placed menu items, and smart search tools can overcome many of the resulting duplications that may arise from such mergings. And, if mergers are planned a little more carefully at the outset, users can be presented an interface with the look and feel of a single digital "mega-library" rather than a collection of smaller ones, each with a different interaction protocol.

Today, even the largest digital libraries are small; while the Library of Congress houses over 100 million "traditional" artifacts, its online counterpart, the National Digital Library, "houses" a few hundred thousand, at most. When digital libraries finally acquire substantial holdings, they will have promise for addressing several important goals and problems of higher education, the first being costs. Costs could drop substantially. From a technical perspective, a document need cost no more than the price of producing it on a nearby high-quality laser printer, which would easily undercut the price of common university texts, not to mention rare volumes.

Of course, publishers are unlikely to tolerate such indiscriminate copying of their property, at least as copyright law now stands. However, by aggregating their acquisitions, digital college libraries are already discovering that they can use their coordinated buying power to negotiate much more effective licensing deals than publishers are willing to offer on books. Digital libraries can improve access to educational material even as they reduce access cost, thereby promising to be a key component in future distance-learning curricula.

Students within a university will enjoy better access to digital materials, in part because they will be able to use them at any place and any time, not just in library study halls; and they will not have to wait for days or weeks until popular titles are returned to the shelf. More interestingly, as digital libraries merge, students can access the very best materials, regardless of their institutional affiliation.

Even if such mergers do not happen officially, students may be able to implement them informally. Today, for example, nothing prevents University of Michigan students on the Web from accessing digital holdings at Stanford, MIT, University of Illinois, or any of the other dozens of online libraries. For that matter, nothing prevents any Internet user-say, an unemployed worker in Detroit or a teenager in Harlem-from perusing these digital documents.

This may not be true for long, however. It is quite easy for universities to put up "firewalls," which permit access only to their students and faculty. Technically easy, yes, but perhaps hard to justify; digital-library resources, unlike books, are simply not "consumed" when used. With well-designed library servers and ample bandwidth, the hundreds of authorised users of a digital library should not notice a thousand or more unofficial users.

All of this would suggest that the best world of all would be one with a single digital library, located at a single site (or perhaps distributed throughout cyberspace), and surrounded by a collection of smart, user-friendly, library tools and software agents to help find digital resources, piece them together into new documents, and share them among students and faculty.

Productive Digital Libraries

For several reasons, this vision of the future is a long way off, even if it is a good one. To begin with, different universities and different communities may simply want to retain different digital documents; local decency laws, as well as informal cultural preferences, will continue to encourage diversity, and sometimes insularity, in digital holdings. Even discounting regional preferences, some important technical hurdles still need to be overcome.

A completely universal digital library presupposes standards for representing the different kinds of multimedia information that make up the digital documents. The de facto standards for WWW homepages (namely, HTML and HTTP) are a good first step in this direction, but they are a long way from being complete. Indeed, closure may be a receding goal, because new data formats and media types are being spawned faster than standards for existing ones are being settled.

It is also important to remember that few of the artifacts now in traditional libraries (so-called legacy materials) have been digitised; they must be included in any digital library that even pretends to supplant a paper-based one. On top of all this, digital materials, no less than paper products, are subject to decay and deterioration. Although the technical problems are substantial, perhaps the biggest obstacles to building digital libraries are legal and institutional. Higher-education institutions have a long history of independence in the way they provide services.

Even if economic and social arguments point toward merging digital libraries, whether universities will enthusiastically embrace changes that might threaten their institutional identity is not clear-especially if they can convince themselves that sharing their knowledge base will lose students, and thus revenue, to competing schools. Finally, copyright problems could kill the development of digital libraries in their infancy. Over decades, copyright law has forged a delicate balance between the interests of publishers and those of consumers, with libraries in the middle. First-sale doctrine permits libraries to lend books without requiring libraries or readers to further compensate publishers and authors.

Similarly, over time, libraries have negotiated extensions of fair-use laws that allow students and faculty to (photo)copy materials without violating copyright. Current copyright law is not particularly generous to consumers, and a direct application of it to digital documents, if possible at all, would certainly not give readers the more-or-less free and unlimited copying privileges that are tacitly assumed in the scenarios we just sketched.

But even these rules would be preferable to some of the revisions of copyright now being drafted with digital materials in mind. If these kinds of changes are enacted, students and faculty will be required to pay each time they skim virtual shelves that hold recent issues of digital periodicals.

Digital Publishers

Publishers, of course, see the threat very differently. To them, the Internet calls up their ultimate nightmare: The U.S. Library of Congress buys one copy of a digital text for its collection, makes the copy available on interlibrary loan to any other library or patron, whereupon, since bits are so easily reproduced, every reader can manufacture his or her own copy with a few mouse clicks. The first sale of a digital book might well be the last.

While admittedly fanciful, this extreme example holds more than a grain of truth. Copyright law can afford to be more generous when built-in barriers-the machinery needed to reproduce tapes, the time and cost of photocopy paper, for instance-provide natural disincentives to duplication. But these disincentives are largely gone with digital products. So, today, most publishers spend as much time defending themselves against the Internet as they do creating products for it.

Over the past few years, this fear has slowly started to transform through a variety of other emotions and actions: uncertain acceptance, careful study, strategic mergers, and hasty exits. Still, recognising a booming educational software market whose retail sales may have climbed as much as 50 percent in 1995 (to over $500 million), traditional publishing houses, together with some fresh competitors, are beginning to sell substantial quantities of new products to higher education.

Conservatism, however, still seems the order of the day, in at least two senses. First, the initial reaction of many large publishers has been to simply follow the lead of the pioneering academics, who are abandoning paper journals in favor of just-in-time electronic versions, following the "if you can't beat them, buy them" strategy: Some small and informal online publishing sites are being acquired by professional publishers. BioMedNet, for example, initially the brain-child of a few researchers, was taken over by Current Science, a small but fast-moving new publishing firm that specialises in value-added electronic products.

Second, while publishers certainly will develop more and better digital products for higher education-BioMedNet has grown from a single digital journal to a rich, online community, for example-the processes by which new titles are created in the future probably will not be much different from what they are now. To find places where information technology is changing the ways in which learning materials are created in a big way, we must look at a much smaller scale: the individual publisher.

IMPACTS OF INTERNET

Consider again the World Lecture Hall, a virtual repository of online course materials. The most prominent feature of the Hall is a large table that organises specific courseware by subject matter. It is much like a standard university course catalog, except that the offerings are full sets of course materials, rather than brief course descriptions.

The Hall also provides tools that allow new courses to be easily searched and added, and a "What's New" link to identify the latest entries (a very valuable resource for frequent browsers, since hundreds of courses already reside at the Hall). The World Lecture Hall demonstrates two very powerful benefits of information technology for education-one already widely touted, the other less so. Relatively familiar is the idea that new technologies encourage individual, home-grown production.

In higher education, we have seen such production in electronic journals that bypass traditional publication bottlenecks, as well as in online courses constructed by individual faculty almost from scratch, using digital materials. Outside education, the examples are often even more compelling. Today, for example, audio and video desktop publishing puts at one's fingertips the facilities that just a few years ago were available only to large, well-funded professional studios.

Using these tools, small grassroots print-journalists, moviemakers, and record producers are already making significant inroads into markets traditionally dominated by big players. There is no reason to believe that, at least on technical grounds, educational publication and the creation of instructional materials will be immune to these sea changes. The second feature has more to do with the World Lecture Hall itself, and the cooperative curriculum development it can encourage, than with the nature and origins of its constituent online courses.

The Hall attempts to provide a location and supporting tools that will encourage faculty not only to create new online course materials, but to share those materials with others. Because the Hall is implemented as a Web homepage, all materials from a course can be downloaded (a trivial process) from the Hall site (which happens to be in Texas) to the browser's home machine.

Using simple but very powerful digital cut-and-paste tools, this copy can be edited into a new course-possibly for a slightly different topic and audience, and, perhaps also a better product. In any case, the new version can be returned to the World Lecture Hall, adding to the materials available to share with the academic community. Eventually, this kind of chaotic cooperation might lead to a vast collection of digital courses of progressively better quality, as a new set of course creators stands on the shoulders of the current creators.

Individual Publishing

Most home-grown products-whether in the form of videotapes, audio recordings, or Web homepages-suffer from a common problem: Although their creators view them as priceless, few others may. Just as once we were bored to tears by our neighbors' vacation slide shows, today most Web surfers are frustrated by the thousands of homepages that serve only to hide the few gems they seek. In the case of virtual collections such as the World Lecture Hall, it is likely that if potential consumers cannot find quality digital course materials, they will cease browsing this site.

If so, the number of new entries will decrease, and, with fewer shoulders to stand on, the overall quality of offerings is unlikely to improve quickly, if at all. In this future, the World Lecture Hall, far from flourishing, would probably disappear within a few semesters. Whether or not such sites foster a productive community of grassroots publishing in higher education will depend on a number of factors. Luck and good timing may play a role. If, for example, home-grown sites develop strong early products, they may attract the attention and new contributors needed to sustain them through their formative period.

Also, even if quality products exist, they must be easy to find. Internet search engines and smart agents already help consumers locate useful sites and ignore irrelevant ones. Providers also have several means at their disposal to simplify search and improve product quality. Passive tools, such as the World Lecture Hall's table organisation and "What's New" option, help make navigation easier for consumers. Other providers take more active steps, preferring to control the quality of products they include in their collections, rather than just relying on consumers to cut through irrelevant materials with search tools.

One ingenious, simple idea that virtual Yellow Pages are trying is to rely on consumer popularity to organise products and shape the market by letting users rate any business in their database and permit new buyers to see these reviews. Although this strategy has not been applied to educational courseware databases, the implementation would probably be very simple; however, the long-term consequences of using such a quality-management scheme would certainly be far from easy to predict. Taking a more traditional approach, electronic journals such as BioMedNet have instituted formal peer-review procedures.

Similarly, many of the electronic discussion groups on Usenet (the newsgroup side of the Internet) are moderated, rather than uncontrolled. Moderators can play a wide range of roles: reorganising and packaging submitted materials, editing copy, adding commentary, and even censoring contributions outright. All this sounds very much like the value-added functions of traditional publishers. It hardly comes as a surprise, therefore, that publishing firms, seeking to redefine their roles in the digital age, are now seeking partnerships with developers of home-grown online course materials for higher education.

In addition to ensuring quality and packaging of new products, many publishers are planning also to market the courseware, secure copyright agreements, and arrange licensing. Individual publishing on the Internet is so new that it is difficult to determine how significantly it will contribute to the creation of new instruction and learning materials. If it flourishes, however, this innovative approach could speak to several important goals and problems of higher education, such as the need for just-in-time and on-demand learning.

Home-grown publishing is now technically feasible because information technologies greatly simplify constructing, editing, and sharing of documents, which may invite the creation of many low-quality products. But, suitably channeled, high-volume and high-speed production also has its good side. Obviously, the easier it is for individual faculty members to create courseware (or to tailor existing materials into new packages), the more they will be able to offer diverse materials to an expanding and increasingly divergent student population.

Responding to a nearly overwhelming need for remedial instruction, for example, faculty from the California State University system might be able to put together a fresh physics curriculum in short order by combining some of the simpler digital simulations, assignments, and exams from any of the more than 25 physics courses now online in the World Lecture Hall. This same flexibility could permit institutions to build new courseware and learning products that respond to the rapidly changing demands of industry-not, assuming popular predictions are right, a one-time effort.

Former Labor Secretary Robert Reich, among others, claims that workers will need to retool for up to five job changes per career. If so, rapid changes in instructional materials will be the rule for the foreseeable future; and the versatility that new information technologies bring to educational production will be critical for meeting these demands. In short, just as information technology already helps manufacturing and services industries to dramatically shorten production cycles and to help solve the challenge of just-in-time academic publishing, it could enable higher education to meet the demand for just-in-time or on-demand learning.

Viewed broadly, information technologies might change the ways instruction and learning materials are created much as they could alter the ways instruction and learning are delivered: by providing many different kinds of applications, not just one or a few. The applications could speak to a variety of goals and problems in higher education, helping to reduce costs, enrich and diversify course offerings, expand access, and increase responsiveness to industry demands and social needs; and some of the most valuable uses of information technology will not simply improve educational productivity, but will require institutions to consider moderate or extensive structural transformations.

For example, by digitising library holdings, universities can expect to save space, reduce acquisition costs, seamlessly combine multimedia documents with traditional text, and provide students and faculty with a new generation of tools for finding information and organising it into intellectual products. However, although a single university can benefit from digitisation, cross-institutional cooperation may be critical if digital libraries are to make the best-quality materials available to students and to reach the broadest audience. Copyright problems will challenge this kind of library merging, as will barriers between higher-education institutions.

By the same token, smaller, grassroots publishers on the Web, rather than larger, traditional publishing firms, look to be nimbler providers of new digital courseware that will meet changing industry needs. But, at least today, the individual publication process is chaotic, to say the least. In the World Lecture Hall, for instance, faculty often cut and paste new curricula from previous offerings, with little concern for copyright or institutional origin.

This kind of highly informal cross-institutional collaboration has been common in academic research. Nevertheless, in the past, most higher-education institutions have been much more reluctant to share their course offerings, informally or otherwise. So, as with digital libraries, individual academic publishing may stress or even transform existing institutional structures, rather than simply enabling them to operate more productively without fundamental change.

A slightly different way to view all this is that the Internet is beginning to foster new academic and learning communities across the Web, most of which are organising along functional lines: developing courseware, conducting research, sharing curricula, for instance. Common interests and expertise are much more important in defining these communities than is distance, an impediment that cheap, high-bandwidth connectivity largely erases.

For similar reasons, most cyberspace communities tend to ignore institutional boundaries when those boundaries interfere with emerging functional interests. These forces are beginning to give rise to new communities of practice that, at the very least, crisscross previous structures and may even erode old higher-education structures while building new ones.

6

Electronic Documents

Electronic publications cover the rapidly increasing area of publications that require a computer to be used to access the information that they contain. They can be documents distributed free of charge or obtained by purchase. They are supplied in two forms—Off-line publications and On-line publications. Some electronic publications are not supplied on physical carriers and need to be copied into the libraries' access system and be stored on hard disc stacks, tape streamers or other data storage systems; others are supplied on physical carriers and can be stored on shelves.

Off-line Publications

An off-line publication is an electronic document which is bibliographically identifiable, which is stored in machine readable form on an electronic storage medium. CD-ROM, diskettes or floppy discs and magnetic tapes are examples.

— Off-line monograph eg a CD-ROM encyclopaedia.

— Off-line serial eg a CD-ROM journal.

On-line Publications

An on-line publication is an electronic document which is

bibliographically identifiable, which is stored in machine readable form on an electronic storage medium and which is available on-line. For example—an electronic journal, a World Wide Web page or an on-line database.

— On-line monograph eg. a dictionary on the Web.

— On-line serial eg. an electronic journal on the Web

— On-line resource eg. an organisation's home page.

Electronic publications can be original electronic publications, but they can also be the digitised version of a written or printed document. For many collections, most of the electronic publications will be the digitised version of a written or printed document in their possession.

Examples include the CD-ROM of the National Library in Prague which contains several manuscripts and other documents, the Saint Sophia Project from Bulgaria, the Radziwill Chronicle, the Sana'a Manuscripts and the Memoria de Iberoamerica. The producers and publishers of electronic publications can be traditional publishers who expand into new areas of publishing. It can also be newly established content providers, especially in case of the new publications on the World Wide Web, who only offer on-line electronic publishing.

In addition, some companies specialise in CD-ROM publishing. Nowadays, most publications are written, edited and formatted using word processors and desk-top-publishing software. The printed version of the journal or the monograph is derived from the electronic form.

Audiovisual Material and an Electronic Publication

Multimedia publications are now produced which contain a mixture of material e.g. a biography, a bibliography, stills, animation, video and sound. It sometimes becomes difficult to distinguish between an audiovisual document and an electronic publication related to text. For example, a movie with subtitling is audiovisual—a CD of Michael Jackson with a video clip consisting of moving images is considered to be an audio CD.

A CD-ROM which contains a biography, a bibliography, texts of the songs, some sound, video and photos is considered to be a multimedia CD-ROM publication. In short, an electronic publication must contain a considerable amount of text before a library will take it on deposit. Some libraries also take audiovisual publications into deposit. e.g. Die Deutsche Bibliothek in Frankfurt am Main in Germany.

Virtual Information

The term Electronic Documents or, as they are sometimes called, Virtual Information refers to the modern methods of transmitting documents between individuals, primarily text-based documents—the equivalents of letters and memoranda—by electronic means ie. without the use of paper. Many of the actual and potential problems created by electronic documents are similar to those created by electronic publications. The documents, while stored on a physical carrier somewhere and easily accessible to a small group of people including the author, are, nethertheless, difficult for an archivist to obtain access to and preserve.

The documents include E-Mail messages and computer files held on personal computers. When electronic documents are stored, it is on physical carriers used by other types of documents. The main factor that differentiates electronic documents from other documents is the method of transmission. The first, and major, problem in the preservation of electronic documents is to gain access to them and discover what exists. This can only be done with the active support of the institution and its staff. If the institution has a PC network, the problem of access can be eased.

Since many of the E-Mail messages between staff are likely to be trivial and, perhaps, somewhat embarrassing if read by others than the author and the intended recipients, it is essential to ensure that everyone is aware that the archive will be periodically reviewing both formal files and messages held in the central file server to select material that is worth preserving. Once access is gained, the material can be subject to standard selection criteria and the chosen information copied into the archive's data storage system. The long term preservation of the information can then be part of the archive's strategy for documents in general.

Factors of Acquiring Electronic Documents

Selection: Research is being carried out by many archives and libraries into the best methods to give access to electronic materials in the very long term. Because of the sheer quantity of material being produced, particularly for access via the World Wide Web, selection is essential. Many archives and libraries use the existing selection criteria for printed materials for electronic materials as well. The contents of the document are the relevant factors for selection and not the medium. This means that the physical carrier, the hardware and the software used are not relevant for the selection process. Local policy defines the criteria for selection e.g. in Germany audiovisual material is included in the national bibliography, in some other countries it is not.

Acquisition and Registration: Off-line publications can often come to the library as printed publications. Obviously, when the library starts collecting off-line publications, the publishers have to be notified. In the

Netherlands, where deposit is done on voluntary basis, it is important that the publishers are kept informed about the new selection criteria. In France, the law defines what publications are to be submitted. On-line publications require a new form of co-operation. The publication has to be transmitted from the host system to the library via the network.

Selected documents are either ordered, transferred automatically by the publisher or harvested by the library with a harvester application. For on-line documents, acquisition means the physical migration of the document from the host-system to the depository system. The publisher/producer or administrator (for archives) needs to be involved in this process. It is necessary to register documents when they are received by the library. This requires the exchange of bibliographic information (pre-publishing information) between the depository library and publisher (for archives this will be between the governmental institution and the archive), preferably before acquisition. The registration of incoming documents should be activated on arrival.

Installation: It is necessary to install the electronic publication so it can be viewed and described by the librarian. For on-line documents, a connection to the host-system is required; off-line documents have to be physically installed on a workstation.

Description of the Document: Cataloguing systems for electronic documents are still the subject of much debate. Various groups are discussing how to describe an electronic document. The existing book-based systems such as MARC and its variants do not fully describe these new formats.

Metadata: Electronic publications offer an opportunity to automate part of the production of a catalogue.

Bibliographic data can be retrieved from the electronic publication itself, e.g. from the table of contents (TOC). A research project of the European Commission, BIBLINK, is studying how data can be exchanged between publisher and library in an automated way. The Dublin Core defines the fields that are necessary to support adequate bibliographic description of a Web page.

The Dublin Core has received significant support, particularly from North America and including some publishers. A threat that may ultimately make it unacceptable, is that the Dublin Core contains too many features requiring definition at the national level or that require a large maintenance overhead.

Unique Identification: In the international book trade, the unique identification numbers ISBN (International Standard Book Number) and ISSN (International Standard Serial Number) are widely used to uniquely identify a certain version of a monograph or serial publication. ISBN and ISSN are also used for CD-ROMs and on-line publications like electronic journals. However, these numbers are not designed for electronic publications and a proposal was, therefore, made for a Digital Object Identifier (DOI). The DOI is designed by Association of American Publishers and the Corporation for National Research Initiatives.

Authenticity and Integrity: Some electronic publications can easily be changed. What guarantee is there that the bibliographic description defines exactly the version which is stored? And will it still do so after the lapse of several hundred years and the migration to other carriers and formats. This is still a very tricky area. Several methods are being considered, e.g. time stamps, encryptions and watermarks. But it must be said that the final solution for this issue has yet to be found.

De-installation: After the bibliographical and technical description the electronic publication must be removed from the hard disk on the computer and an on-line session must be closed. This activity has generated new information which should be included to the descriptive record.

Migration, Storage, Conversion and Emulation: Other factors that have to be considered when collecting electronic documents include the following:

— Migration of the electronic content from the original carrier to the physical storage of the depository system, including migration quality control and duplication for backup.

— The physical storage system will probably use different types of media with different access speeds, e.g. hard disc (very fast), magneto-optical (fast), tape (slow). This requires sophisticated software to monitor the use of documents and to shift documents from tape to discs and vice versa.

— Pathfinder is a storage records the physical locations of all the files in a document and makes the file map available to the search engine.

Conversion and Emulation: Do you have to convert the format of the document to a new format, or do you have to design a system in which the document is stored in the original format? Emulation software enables the document stored in the original format to be viewed using the new hardware and software.

These techniques are concerned with preservation and final solutions have not yet been found. Increasing speed of technological innovation, new publishing techniques, InterNet and the present lack of standards are a few examples of the uncertainties in which the manager of a depository system must work. There is no proven solution for these systems, large vendors have build systems for data-warehousing and data-mining, although they still lack structured indexing and large scale preservation solutions needed by libraries and archives

Long Term Availability and Access for End Users

— *Indexing:* Descriptive information is indexed for use within the search engine of the depository system. This engine can be part of the pathfinder software or can be a separate existing library system's OPAC module, to be defined locally. To find the right compromise between (the user's) indexing requirements and the technical possibilities is very complicated.

— *Access:* Access to electronic publications by end users must be clearly defined. At present, most access is "on-site" but, when agreements are made with the owners of the information, remote access may be possible.

As with the deposit for printed publications, electronic deposit collections should be used as "collections of last resort". Libraries can, however, give access when agreements are reached with publishers and authors.

— *Copyright Issues, Authors and Publishers:* It is obvious that it is very important that the digital archives and libraries discuss restrictions on access and availability with publishers and authors when this is appropriate.

Usage of Standards: There are many relevant standards for electronic publications. The European Commission has launched an initiative, OII (Open Information Interchange), as part of the IMPACT2 programme. The aim of the OII initiative is to promote the awareness and use of standards for the exchange of information in electronic form. The target audience are developers and providers of information products and services, as well as end-users.

Standards can be purchased from international standard offices and many countries have an organisation which translates and distributes the standards. For more information visit the Commission's Web site where copies of publications on standards can be found. For the preservation of electronic publications a variety of standards are relevant. These include standards on hardware, operating systems (Windows, MS-DOS, UNIX), physical carriers (CD-ROM, WORM, DAT, diskettes, magnetic tapes), application programmes like wordprocessors, databases, spread sheets and formats like MARC, SGML, HTML etcetera.

Printed publications like monographs and serials are no longer available on the market permanently. After a relatively short time, a specific edition of a monograph can be difficult to find in a book shop. It may be possible to order from a large distributor or even the publisher. With off-line electronic publications it is exactly the same. The publishers are no longer interested in keeping publications available when there is no commercial interest in the products. This may be understandable from the market point of view but is still unfortunate.

In addition, publishers often do not have a full archive of their own publications. It is very important, therefore, that as soon as possible after the publication date a document should be selected, described and made available by a public body like a national archive or a national library.

7

Networked Digital Library

Digital libraries containing resources that are helpful to learners will reduce costs and promote mutual understanding, as well as speed up the transfer of knowledge and encourage international collaboration in the academy. Essential properties of such efforts are that they be:

— beneficial, leading to increases in access, learning, collaboration, and understanding;

— sustainable, so they will continue, which follows naturally from becoming an integral part of some regular activity like students pursuing graduate degrees or faculty updating courses on computing;

— scalable, so they will grow and expand without problem, which follows from being highly distributed and being undertaken directly by large numbers of individuals without extra follow-up processing or bottlenecks; and

— automatible, so technological aids actually reduce labor and cost relative to prior approaches, especially when viewed end-to-end.

In this chapter we can see two such digital library initiatives, the Networked Digital Library of Theses and

Dissertations (NDLTD) and the Computer Science Teaching Center (CSTC). The first relates mainly to graduate education and research while the latter is particularly focussed on undergraduate learners, especially in connection with US National Science Foundation (NSF) efforts toward a national digital library for Science, Mathematics, Engineering and Technology Education (SMETE).

Networked Digital Library of Theses and Dissertations

The NDLTD is open for all universities as well as other supporting institutions to join. As of July 1998 it included three national efforts, in the USA, Australia, and Portugal. Members are drawn not only from the United States but also from Canada, Germany, Korea, Mexico, Portugal, Russia, Singapore, and South Africa—with other members likely to join in scores of universities around the world.

In November 1987, in Ann Arbor, Michigan, USA, the first public meeting occurred about the use of electronic document processing methods, in particular SGML (Standard Generalised Markup Language), for theses and dissertations. The meeting was hosted by UMI, and included representatives from the University of Michigan, SoftQuad, ArborText, and Virginia Tech. Over the next year, Virginia Tech funded and worked with SoftQuad to develop a DTD (Document Type Definition) for theses and dissertations.

This has been refined and used for a small number of dissertations, and is documented at a Virginia Tech WWW site which gives extensive instructions so students can create Electronic Theses and Dissertations (ETDs). SGML-based ETDs are highly desirable, and should become feasible in the next few years as XML becomes popular and well supported by producers of word processing software.

That is one of the goals agreed upon in a 1994 meeting in Blacksburg, Virginia, USA attended by representatives of a number of universities interested in ETDs. The other goal, which became feasible by 1995, is submission of ETDs using Adobe's Portable Document Format (PDF), which affords a fully-rendered and directly readable version of student research results. Once it was clear that these goals could be met, and once funding was secured from the Southeastern Universities Research Association and from the U.S. Department of Education for piloting the concept of ETDs, the National Digital Library of Theses and Dissertations was launched.

Since then there has been extensive news coverage on this project, which has attracted a good deal of interest. However, since some parts of the news stories are misleading, usually overly sensational or controversial so as to attract attention, it is important to give below a more accurate description. Also, because the project has expanded in a short period into an international initiative, now called "Networked" instead of "National", that could provide important benefits to scholarship in Russia and around the world, it is appropriate to explain the goals, problems faced, solutions and plans of NDLTD.

The goals of NDLTD include:

— to enhance graduate education;

— to help ensure that all future scholars are information literate, with skills to produce electronic documents and use digital libraries, as well as some basic understanding of issues relating to intellectual property rights;

— to improve the availability and content of theses and dissertations;

— to help universities unlock more of their intellectual resources;

— to serve as a model digital library project that is not only beneficial but also scalable and sustainable; and

— to serve as a model project demonstrating how universities can collaborate.

In addition to university-level goals, many students have their own goals regarding ETDs. Electronic documents can simply be the electronic version of a document designed for paper distribution, saving students the cost associated with photocopying and the hassles related to shipping if the student is not on campus but does have access to the Internet for file transmission. Of greater importance may be the goal of having works quickly and widely disseminated. Since ETDs often include a student's resume, and represent some of their finest work, rapid distribution may help students secure jobs or quickly become well known in their fields. This seems quite feasible, since the rate of distribution may increase by a factor of 100 or more when electronic instead of paper means are used.

While there were about 37K accesses to the Virginia Tech collection in 1996, there were 248K in 1997 and 218K in January-May 1998. That amounts to a growth in average daily rate from 102 to 685 to 1432. The number of PDF files downloaded (approximately equal to the number of full ETDs downloaded, since most are made up of a single PDF file) rose from about 5K in 1996 to 73K in 1997 to 118K in the first part of 1998.

Even more exciting to some students is the possibility of an ETD being more expressive than traditional works. Electronic documents may, if the faculty members involved permit, include color, multimedia, hypertext links, data files, and other valuable resources usually only described in paper publications. Students can upload files for network access that previously could only be shared on CD-ROM or diskette. Experience at Virginia Tech indicates that roughly two-thirds of submissions have multimedia components. Thus, there are works with audio and video files, Java programmes, a tutorial for the AuthorWare system, and VRML files for chemical structures.

Some faculty members are particularly interested in improving the quality of theses and dissertations. The University of South Florida has an active writing center that hopes to boost the quality of the writing. Electronic tools to help diagnose and suggest fixes to problems, as well as systems that enhance collaboration with writing experts or scholars in the discipline, may be of value. A key idea in NDLTD is to have students carry out the full activity, so they learn by doing. Besides preparing and submitting their ETDs to NDLTD, they also should learn about their intellectual property rights.

Another key dimension of the approach that is taken by NDLTD members is for the university to, according to its local policies and structure, develop a climate and infrastructure that supports the efforts of students to prepare ETDs, as well as handling the requirements of the graduate school and library. This often occurs in stages, beginning with the formation of a representative committee, followed by a small group of staff adapting the tools and WWW sites developed at Virginia Tech. Next there is a pilot study by a department or center that has particular interest, voluntary submissions going on for some period to spread the concept to those with greatest aptitude, and then a well-publicised shift to requiring submissions, sometimes initially just for a particular college. Since

— theses and dissertations are approved by different groups at different universities (e.g., by each college in cases where there is no graduate school);

— providing assistance to graduate students is handled by varying groups (e.g., a computing center or library help service); and

— library processing varies (e.g., regarding cataloging, preserving, and locating theses—in a departmental vs. college vs. central library);

— then it follows that there may be differing approaches to handling of training, stocking and supporting labs with word processing software, and assisting with multimedia capture and presentation.

Some of the most challenging problems associated with digital libraries relate to social or cultural concerns. Since the aim with NDLTD is to have a profound effect on scholarly publishing, university sharing of information, dissemination of knowledge, and graduate education, it is not surprising that people have voiced concerns or identified problem areas. Those working on NDLTD accept the challenge of developing model solutions to such concerns and problems, like those described below.

Cultures and Languages

One set of issues deals with variations between cultures and languages. Since theses and dissertations are written by graduate students worldwide, usually in their native language, often describing or set in the context of local culture, and can more effectively carry their message when multimedia content is included, ETDs will vary regarding language, cultural portrayal, and use of multimedia forms. Fortunately, there are systems for multilingual searching and mechanisms for handling multimedia information.

Similarly, universities already handle cataloging, indexing, search, storing, distributing and preserving of paper theses and dissertations. These can form the basis for similar activities with ETDs. These challenges can be met by each university operating autonomously, using appropriate information technology for its local efforts, and cooperating with others in NDLTD to ensure interoperability.

Universities involved in NDLTD often elect to adapt the WWW, automation, and training materials developed at Virginia Tech to suit their local culture, policies, and procedures. Any of a large number of search tools can be deployed by a participating institution so it can become part of the simple "federated search" system developed at Virginia Tech and accessible at the central collection site. For universities wishing to afford access to their ETD collections, local search engines are of value. Virginia Tech used the Free WAIS software initially, which is adequate for the task, but then shifted to the more powerful OpenText system that was licensed for general searching efforts around campus.

OCLC has donated a copy of their SiteSearch software, which can provide another alternative. SiteSearch supports Z39.50, which enables access through a variety of clients and which affords users varying views of distributed collections. It also can be adapted to enable federated search of all ETD repositories in parallel, with client or gateway merging of results from remote sites. The University of Virginia has taken the initiative on adapting the Dienst system to use for ETDs. Work is underway at Virginia Tech to use IBM Digital Library to afford access, since it has strong support for protecting intellectual property.

When a university joins NDLTD, it begins to develop infrastructure to support its students as they learn about electronic publishing, digital libraries, intellectual property rights, and other key concerns necessary for them to function effectively in the Information Age. This often includes a small WWW site, typically adapted from the pages in use at Virginia Tech. If students use the online WWW-based submission software provided by Virginia Tech to upload the files that make up their ETDs, the university may support that as well. Typically it provides storage of the files while their work is being checked for conformity with graduate policies and is being cataloged for library handling.

If the university elects to itself make ETDs available, some type of digital library support is needed too. Probably the most elaborate infrastructure involved in the ETD initiative is provided by institutions encouraging the use of multimedia content in theses or dissertations. Devices for capturing, converting and manipulating images, video, audio, virtual reality environments, etc. can be provided by libraries, computing organisations, or in a variety of places around each campus. At Virginia Tech this is handled through the New Media Center in the Library as well as in a number of computer laboratories.

At a more basic level, students need word processing software to create their documents. Adobe's Acrobat products support the handling of Portable Document Format (PDF) files, the format usually chosen for ETD submission. Use of SGML is encouraged, aided by Virginia Tech's document type definition (DTD) for ETD-ML, the markup scheme which has been repeatedly refined to be easy to use and yet powerful enough to capture the important metadata and structure of ETDs. Efforts are underway at the University of Virginia and the University of Michigan to apply the guidelines of the Text Encoding Initiative and their DTDs for students willing to include much more extensive markup.

Virginia Tech will have guidelines by 1999, when XML solutions will become feasible for large numbers of students, so authors working with Microsoft Word and other packages can export their ETDs into that emerging archival form. In addition to hardware and software to support NDLTD, Virginia Tech also has a rich network infrastructure, including a vBNS (high speed Internet research and education backbone) connection through "Net.Work Virginia," the statewide ATM network with over 220 nodes that it runs and which includes educational institutions all over the Commonwealth.

Since Virginia Tech has offered to provide archival support for NDLTD members in the short term, through an IBM-donated server with four terabytes of storage, it is useful to have such comprehensive infrastructure, though that is certainly not required for NDLTD members. Indeed, since UMI has a business activity that provides preservation and access services for theses and dissertations, involving paper, microforms, and now electronic services, institutions can elect to just support student submission and local approvals, paying UMI to handle other matters. The NDLTD Steering Committee is pleased that both UMI and OCLC have indicated interest in long-term archival support, and encourages an open competitive environment in which a variety of efforts evolve to maintain and expand access to ETDs.

Access and Publishing

More serious concerns arise in connection with publishers. Some researchers argue that ETDs are a separate and unique genre, which should operate independently of other types of publications. Thus, an ETD is much longer and more detailed than a paper that might appear in a conference proceedings or journal. Similarly, a humanities dissertation usually goes through substantial refinement and enhancement before appearing through a university press as a monograph. The first solution they have adopted regarding confusion about affording widespread access is to work with publishers.

Seconnd is, they developed an Approval Form that is signed by students and their faculty committee. It allows them to:

— restrict access completely, in case a patent is sought;

— restrict access to campus, in case a publisher requires an article to appear in their publication before the related ETD becomes available through NDLTD;

— restrict access to part of the work, while affording open access to the rest, for cases when one chapter or other component is similar to a journal submission; or

— allow free worldwide access.

The Approval Form protects students from being penalised by publishers. However, it is very easy to just restrict access by checking a box, which then substantially delays or reduces the number of people who will read an ETD. Further work with publishers on policies, and social pressure from the increasing number of universities in NDLTD to allow ETDs to be more freely shared, is needed.

In the future, NDLTD will continue to help universities work together, with the aim of rapid scale up. All research universities have theses and dissertations, and all colleges have bachelor theses and other major papers. These parts of the "gray literature" are largely ignored and disappear from view, except in the case of about fifty thousand dissertations per year in North America. With hundreds of thousands of students involved in the creation of such documents, often spending months or years in preparing them, there is strong motivation for making them more accessible.

With significant faculty time and other university resources going into the development of these works, there is an incentive at the university level to proceed with NDLTD, especially since it ensures some basic level of electronic publishing skills among graduates, and reduces overall costs. With these motivations in place, and with a number of universities interested in helping others ensure that ETDs increase in quality as well as quantity (e.g., through writing enhancement and inclusion of multimedia components), it appears that there are incentives for universities to collaborate.

Since there are few other venues in which universities worldwide can cooperate and all benefit, and since working on NDLTD will ensure that participating universities develop at least a basic infrastructure in the digital library arena, it appears that NDLTD may be a good vehicle for both university cooperation at the international level and a means for the digital library field to advance. Further, it should be noted that since the digital library field is new, and since the systems and services are still largely prototypes, there is considerable room for evolution. This actually fits in well with the development of NDLTD, which is naturally gated by the rate of joining (which can be done by part or all of a university, with flexibility to begin with only a pilot or optional programme), the training efforts on local campuses, and the implementation of services by different institutions.

Since universities can start small, and since the collection is still in its early growth phase, there is time for additional funding and research investigations to be launched. This is valuable, since requirements are just becoming obvious, and prototypes as well as evaluation efforts are in their early stages. It is clear that we have many challenges, regarding training students about digital libraries, working with publishers to allow an increase in access, developing better archiving mechanisms (e.g., using XML), and enhancing search services (with better multilingual, multimedia, and federated search capabilities). Many of these improvements will arise more rapidly if there is worldwide involvement in this global enterprise.

Computer Science Teaching Center

The Computer Science Teaching Center (CSTC) was launched early in 1998 through funding from the National Science Foundation and ACM Education Committee to improve teaching and learning in the computing field. Like NDLTD, it is open to all, and hopefully will expand and improve in upcoming years.

One thread of interest in digital libraries in the USA began in 1991 with a white paper authored by Lesk, McGill, and Fox that recommended an electronic library to support undergraduate learning; this thread continued through late 1993 when the NSF/DARPA/NASA Digital Libraries Initiative (DLI) was called for. As DLI proceeded over the 4 year period starting in 1994, simultaneous with the emergence of the WWW and the widespread growth of the Internet, the NSF Division of Undergraduate Education (DUE) became increasingly interested in the effects of information technology on Science, Mathematics, Engineering and Technology Education (SMETE).

DUE's advisory committee called for significant reform and use of technology, including developing new systems to support learning. In 1997, DUE sponsored a workshop to see if indeed a digital library should be developed to support SMETE. Based on the recommendations from that meeting, a second workshop was help in July 1998 to clarify the users and scope, develop further plans, and prepare a prioritised feature list for the national digital library.

The core of the charge to the group of almost 100 attendees, which included students but was mostly made up of educators and educational reformers, was to increase access to digital materials for SMETE and to improve their quality. Meanwhile, some related projects, like CSTC, were funded by DUE. These will apply digital library technology to help with undergraduate learning, and should provide examples or early prototypes of the future SMETE library.

The Computer Science Teaching Center (CSTC) combines a number of streams of educational innovation. At Virginia Tech, an NSF CISE Education Infrastructure (EI) project "Interactive Learning with a Digital Library in Computer Science" (http://ei.cs.vt.edu) that ran over the period 1993-98 developed tools and courseware which led to over 10 million accesses by summer 1998. This ongoing effort provides a base of materials to feed into CSTC. At the College of New Jersey, work has been proceeding for several years to construct a repository of laboratory support information to help with computing courses.

At University of Illinois, Springfield, a collection of visualisations and visualisation tools has been growing to facilitate learning about computer science. In addition, another DUE-funded project for "Curriculum Resources in Interactive Multimedia" (CRIM), led by Virginia Tech and The George Washington University, provides another stream of resources to help with teaching about interactive multimedia. These four streams form the initial core of CSTC. Ideas and efforts toward CSTC include:

1. developing a digital library as a distributed system based at several locations, each focussing on a particular topical area or pedagogical goal;
2. encouraging interested parties, who are leaders in their field and who want to build such a distributed library, to launch and support a center in their area of expertise (e.g., laboratories, visualisation, interactive multimedia);
3. having each center take stock of what is available in their subject domain, both commercially and as free- or share-ware, and creating a set of pointers, preferably along with cataloging and browsing support, so those interested in the area have a place to start exploration;
4. developing a worldwide mechanism for collecting and reviewing new submissions for CSTC, so at least a portion of the content is peer-reviewed;
5. connecting with the research community so that new results, especially in the form of demonstrations given at conferences, flow naturally into pedagogically useful resources for education;
6. starting with CRIM, and possibly spreading to other areas, having pairs or larger groups of institutions explicitly form teams to help with developing, generalising, porting, and packaging high quality materials, involving not only the site that creates an item, but also sites that wish to adapt and adopt it;
7. approaching appropriate professional associations, e.g., ACM, to launch some type of electronic journal in connection with CSTC, so that authors of courseware can gain the benefit of having a publication as a result of their efforts, reviewers can obtain credit as they would for reviewing articles, and those engaged in

collection and handling of submissions can achieve the status of journal editors;

8. having a central site, initially at Virginia Tech, perhaps later moving to the ACM Digital Library, for access to the emerging collection; and

9. integrating this effort into the emerging SMETE library.

It is hoped that CSTC will lead to significant improvement in CS education by ensuring that teachers and students can find and adapt high quality materials that support specific learning objectives. Once CSTC becomes widely used, and is established as an essential part of the infrastructure supporting formal and informal learning about computing, it should evolve into a sustainable and beneficial enterprise.

Establishing CSTC in particular, and the SMETE library in general, requires facing a number of challenges. This effort is a significant innovation, and will affect both the publishing and learning practices now prevalent; related changes in the world of publishing over the ages have been highly influential in the world of research and scholarship but now may lead to even greater upheaval.

8

Exploring Web Resources

The first web pages emerged in that faraway era of the early 1990s. Email and the Internet were already becoming well known but the web, which like email uses the Internet's global computer network to share information in commonly agreed-upon ways, had its start among physicists only in 1991. It moved into the mainstream in 1993 when the National Center for Supercomputing Applications (NCSA) at the University of Illinois released Mosaic, an easy-to-use graphical web browser that ran on most standard computers.

Between mid-1993 and mid-1995 the number of servers-the computers that house websites-jumped from 130 to 22,000. Even with the user-friendly Mosaic encouraging a major expansion of this new medium, only a few historians ventured out on the web frontier. Many of the pioneers already had some technical interests or background. In November 1994 Morris Pierce, an engineer who had recently earned a history Ph.D., created one of the first departmental websites for the University of Rochester. It "seemed like a natural thing to do," he recalls.

George Welling already worked in a department of humanities computing, which the University of Groningen (Netherlands) had created in 1986. In the fall of 1994,

Welling developed a course in computer skills for American history students and asked them to construct an American Revolution website. Other History Web pioneers came to the medium out of experience with earlier Internet applications, particularly email. In the late 1980s, Joni Makivirta, a student at the University of Jyvaskyla, Finland started an online history discussion list because he noticed lists on other topics and thought a history list would allow him "to get ideas from professional historians around the world" for his master thesis.

The participants included George Welling, Thomas Zielke, who later took over the list, Richard Jensen, who went on to found H-Net in 1993, Don Mabry, a Latin American historian at Mississippi State University, and Lynn Nelson, a medievalist at the University of Kansas. In 1991, Mabry-responding to the difficulty of circulating large documents via email-began to make available primary sources and other materials of interest to historians via "anonymous FTP"-a "file transfer protocol" that allows anyone with an Internet connection to download the files to their own computers.

Nelson created his own site and then had the idea of linking together the emerging set of history FTP sites into HNSource using Gopher, a hierarchical, menu-driven system for navigating the Internet that was much more popular than the web in the early 1990s. In September 1993, just after Mosaic was released, Nelson made HNSource available through the new web protocols, and it became one of the first if not the very first historical site on the web.

In the 1980s and early 1990s, the most intense energy in digital history centered not on the possibilities of online networks but rather on fixed-media products like laser disks and CD-ROM. In 1982, the Library of Congress began its Optical Disk Pilot Project, which placed text and images from its massive collections on laser disks and later CD-ROM. With a large amount of material already in digital form, the library could quickly take advantage of the newly emerging web. In 1992, it started to offer its exhibits through FTP sites. Two years later, the library posted its first web-based collection, Selected Civil War Photographs.

Around the time that these early settlers carved out primitive digital history homesteads, the first signs emerged that this new frontier might feature more than noncommercial exchange. In October 1994 Marc Andreessen and some of his colleagues who had developed Mosaic at the government-funded NCSA released the first version of a commercially funded browser they called Netscape. Within months, Mosaic was, as they say, history, and Netscape was king of the World Wide Web. The Netscape era saw the History Web come into its own.

In mid-1995, when one of us co-wrote the first published guide to the web for historians in the American Historical Association's (AHA) Perspectives, it announced, "the explosion in Web sites has brought with it an explosion in materials relevant to historians." Earlier that year, the Center for History and New Media (CHNM) had helped the venerable AHA launch its website; by that summer forty-five history departments had posted home pages.

The online presence of the AHA and the Library of Congress provided an official imprimatur to the History Web. But in those early years, amateurs, not professional historical organizations, provided the crucial energy for much of its growth. Starting in 1995, for example, Larry Stevens, a telephone company worker from Newark, Ohio, established a series of websites on Ohio in the Civil War. The sites combined his two hobbies of history and computers, and, he explained, he "decided to carve a niche into the net before the big boys, aka Ohio Historical Society, Ohio State University, etc., entered the field."

Since the mid-1990s, the History Web has spun its threads with astonishing speed. In 2004, the same search yields 640,000 hits. In the fall of 1996, we did some additional history searches with what we thought were even more remarkable results-200 hits for the Civil War General George B. McClellan and 300 for the Socialist Eugene V. Debs. Eight years later, those same searches would overwhelm the web researcher with 97,000 and 18,000 hits.

Even by 1996 the "walking city" that was the History Web a year earlier had become a sprawling megalopolis that no one person could fully explore. Yahoo counted 873 U.S. history websites in an incomplete census that fall. But seven years later, an even less complete tally returned almost ten times as many American history websites. These results reveal a deep and wide fascination with history among the web-browsing public.

Mapping the History Web

Despite the enormity of Yahoo's current history web directory, a cursory glance reveals its incompleteness. For example, it only lists 218 of the more than1,200 history department web pages. Just thirteen online courses and syllabi make their way into the Yahoo directory; yet probably more than 15,000 history syllabi are publicly available on the web. Yahoo catalogs 888 Civil War websites, whereas the United States Civil War Center has 8,000 links in its directory.

Yahoo's web directory is becoming something of a historical artifact. In the first five years of the web Yahoo was one of the dominant websites because it added the librarian's touch of classification and order to a confusing hodgepodge of sites. Now Google's rapid search of the raw mass of disorganized, heterogeneous web pages has replaced, by a tremendous margin, Yahoo's tidy directory as the leading referrer of web visitors. The brute force of computer algorithms has proven far more useful than any human cataloging.

But neither the human-created directories nor the machine-based search engine capture all of the History Web. Much of the web has moved into databases (the "deep web") that search engines have trouble accessing because they require some input from the visitor-a word or phrase-to call up their contents. Google searches on "George McClellan" don't turn up the 500 references, including letters, photos, speeches, and sheet music, within the 8-million-item American Memory collections at the Library of Congress.

In addition, only paying customers can access vast precincts of the History Web, especially those containing secondary sources and even major collections of primary sources. The most careful Google searcher will not locate the 170 references to McClellan in scholarly articles provided online through JSTOR, a subscription database gated off from the public web. And while MIT leads the charge for "open courseware," many universities keep their syllabi locked behind the doors of commercial programs like WebCT and Blackboard, thus making their educational materials unavailable to the broader world.

The History Web has become so sprawling that some history websites concentrate solely on steering perplexed ramblers through the thicket. The World-Wide Web Virtual

Library's History Index, begun by Lynn Nelson in 1993, has evolved into a network of two hundred different gateways and more than 10,000 links with volunteers taking responsibility for developing lists on particular topics (e.g., historical journals or ancient Greece).

Others have developed more specialized gateways focusing on particular topics or audiences. Many of the gateways have struggled with the problems of keeping up with the proliferating numbers of sites and sorting the wheat from the chaff. Six of the nine gateways to U.S. history listed on the Virtual Library's History Index are dead or out of date, perhaps reflecting the Sisyphean task taken on by their editors. In response, some sites have emerged that emphasize qualitative filtering such as our own History Matters: The U.S. Survey Course Online and World History Matters, or Best of History Web Sites organized by Thomas Daccord, a high school history teacher.

Comprehensive and clear categorization of the History Web has proven elusive. Yahoo and many other directories take the most conventional approach, dividing listings by region, topic, and time period. Such divisions make clear that the History Web's composition, in part, follows obvious patterns of economic and political dominance. For example, Yahoo counts 1,352 sites in British history but only 7 on Uganda. Popular history preferences clearly take precedence over professional concerns.

Yahoo lists almost 3,000 genealogy sites and 900 on the Civil War but lacks separate categories for cultural, social, and intellectual history, three of the largest areas of interest among members of the AHA. After having placed most history websites in geographic, topical, or temporal categories, Yahoo's cataloguers-many of them trained as librarians-then throw up their hands at the eclecticism of the History Web and dump the remains under a catchall heading of "Additional History Categories," which includes everything from "Archives and Bibliographies" to "Shopping and Services."

The History Web is both more and less than a good historical library. It has spotty coverage in some areas that have well developed historical literatures. But it provides rich information on topics- African-American heritage tours and popular appropriations of historical figures like FDR among them-that most libraries don't touch upon. One obvious division involves the types of authors.

Because the web allows everyone to be a publisher at a remarkably low cost, amateurs and enthusiasts have a much more prominent place online than they do in print. Not only has the web called into existence a new group of grassroots historians but those non-academic authors have acquired a much more public voice than they had before.

Nevertheless, Larry Stevens's fear about the "big guys" muscling in has proven prescient. Although the number of amateur sites remains larger than those coming from professional historians or historical organizations (museums, libraries, archives), the weight of web traffic has swung in more established directions.

The sites ranked as most popular by Yahoo generally come from universities, government agencies (e.g., the Library of Congress or the National Park Service), or corporations. The entry of large corporations into the History Web creates two further distinctions-between commercial and noncommercial sites and between gated sites and open access.

So far, the presence of commercial history websites

within the public web has been less prominent than many assumed in the era of the Internet gold rush that began shortly after Netscape's stock price went through the roof. Discovery Communications sunk more than $10 million into a site that prominently featured history. Today, it presents only historical material closely related to its cable programs.

Even the original content that it expensively created in 1996 has disappeared. After the dot-com boom fizzled, the companies presenting history online were primarily those selling history as adjuncts of more traditional "bricks and mortar" businesses. Most prominent are the History Channel website and HistoryNet, which is owned by Primedia, the publisher of a stable of such popular history magazines as Civil War Times as well as the owner of About.com, which provides online guides to a variety of subjects, including history.

Both sites reflect the advantages and disadvantages of most popular history-solid writing and production values, but a tendency to avoid controversy or strong interpretations and to focus on topics like war, technology, and entertainment-not surprising, since these sites largely support businesses that emphasize these topics.

The greater corporate presence on the History Web is behind closed doors-the "gates" erected by vendors who sell resources to libraries, especially university libraries, who then dispense them to their customers. Global information conglomerates like ProQuest and the Thomson Corporation have developed vast online databases of newspapers, documents, and books that they license to libraries for large fees and are, hence, available only to the patrons of those libraries able to afford the stiff price.

From the perspective of someone who is thinking

about creating their own website, probably the most helpful way to classify history websites is by the types of materials they provide and the functions and audiences they serve. The past decade has seen the emergence of five main genres of history websites that follow pre-existing patterns and categories: archives (containing primary sources); exhibits, films, scholarship, and essays (that is, secondary sources); teaching (directed at students and teachers); discussion (focused on online dialogue); and organizational (providing information about a historical group).

Yet these categories are often loosely followed and frequently blurred. Almost every exhibit site has primary source documents, as do many teaching sites. Few archival sites totally eschew historical interpretation. And a large number of sites seem to defiantly reject the categorizations neatly laid out above. This is particularly true of topical sites that are intent on covering every possible base on a given topic rather than trying to provide a certain kind of resource or serve a specific audience.

More important, it forces the incipient History Web creator to think about genres themselves, what Phil Agre calls the "expectable form that materials in a given medium might take." Genres imply, in Agre's words, "a particular sort of audience and a particular sort of activity" and are "the meeting-point between the process of producing media materials and the process of using them." To pay attention to genre is to think about how what you are doing relates to the audience you are hoping to reach-something less necessary "in the old days, when media were few and their uses evolved slowly," or when they evolved in an ad hoc, organic way.

The newness of the web requires historians to be much more deliberate about what we are doing and why we are doing it. Moreover, thinking about genres focuses your attention on possible models. You may well aspire to break through categories and surpass what has been done previously-ambitions we applaud-but first you need to be familiar with what has been done before and why it was done that way.

Archival Websites

Professional archivists complain that many archival websites are not archives at all because they lack "provenance," that is, a clear history of the custody of a coherent body of materials since their original creation. Instead, their creators have assembled them from diverse sources. But even archivists would consider most (but not all) of the one hundred collections in the Library of Congress's American Memory website "true" archives.

Whatever you call them, taken together these sites are one of the History Web's greatest achievements and one of its most popular destinations. In the early 1990s, the library distributed optical disks of major collections to test sites around the country, and discovered to its surprise that K-12 teachers and students eagerly embraced the digital gifts. In 1994, the library began moving the collections to the web. Less than a decade and more than $60 million later, American Memory had more than 8 million posted items.

Historians around the globe, not just those with physical access to the Library of Congress, may now conduct such investigations, and with a rapidity impossible when searching meant months of manual turning pages. The early success of American Memory and other pioneering web archives sent hundreds of other libraries and archives to work on getting their own collections online. In 1997, for example, the Bibliothèque nationale de France began the Gallica project to put online multimedia documents from the Middle Ages to the early twentieth century.

Dozens of similar web projects have given the History Web a global reach: PictureAustralia presents 600,000 images from 21 cultural agencies; the Digital Imaging Project of South Africa offers the text of 38 anti-apartheid periodicals, the International Dunhuang Project serves up 20,000 digitized images of Silk Road artifacts; and the Nagasaki University Library displays more than 5,000 hand-tinted photographs from the second half of the nineteenth century.

Beyond its own collections, the Library of Congress played an important early role in spreading digital archives in the United States. With a $2 million grant from the midwestern telephone company Ameritech (now SBC), the Library of Congress sponsored a competition from 1996 through 1999 to enable libraries, museums, historical societies, and archives to create digital collections of primary resources.

Twenty-two funded collections on such topics as Chicago Anarchists, the Chinese in California, the Northern Great Plains, and the Florida Everglades now reside within American Memory. Soon other funding sources as well as the sweat equity of individuals brought dozens of other major collections online.

The Academic Affairs Library at the University of North Carolina at Chapel Hill-with support from Ameritech, the National Endowment for the Humanities (NEH), the Institute of Museum and Library Services, and the university itself-created Documenting the American South, which includes six digitization projects drawn primarily from the library's Southern Collections, including massive collections of first-person narratives and Southern literature.

In 1991, Edward Ayers, a leading Southern historian, began work on a book that would compare the experience of two communities on either side of the Mason-Dixon Line during the Civil War, Augusta County in central Virginia and Franklin County in southern Pennsylvania. In 1992 Ayers and literary critic Jerome McGann, who created a massive site about the Pre-Raphaelite poet and painter Dante Gabriel Rossetti, became the institute's first two fellows.

With the aid of a large team of collaborators and a number of grants, Ayers began digitizing the collections that would underlie his book. Initially, they planned to put the projects on stand-alone computers or local networks, but when they saw Mosaic in the fall of 1993 they knew "everything had changed for our digital projects." Other for-profit projects, especially from large information companies like Canada's Thomson Corporation and Michigan-based ProQuest, have made even more massive investments in digitizing the past. For example, Thomson, a "global e-information and solutions company" with close to $8 billion in annual revenues, offers Eighteenth Century Collections Online, which includes "every significant English-language and foreign-language title printed in Great Britain" in the eighteenth century-33 million text-searchable pages and nearly 150,000 titles.

Thomson Gale, a subsidiary of the Thompson Corporation, calls it "the most ambitious single digitization project ever undertaken" and boasts, "we own the 18th century." Those who want their own share must pay handsomely. A university with 18,000 students can spend more than half a million dollars to acquire the full collection-a hefty price, albeit less than the cost of acquiring the original books. ProQuest, formerly the camera company Bell & Howell, goes head-to-head with Thomson in the fight to own the past.

Exhibits, Films, Scholarship, and Essays

The web offers a vast new canvas on which historians can depict and interpret the past, as we have formerly done in scholarly monographs, popular histories, museum exhibits, documentary films, high school classrooms, or family gatherings. Hundreds of thousands of secondary sources have materialized on the web in its short history. Yet while the medium is new, the interpretations are not.

Most digital interpretive historical materials simply translate analog materials like xmuseum exhibits, scholarly articles, and popular essays to the new medium. The much smaller corpus of born-digital historical sites more often originate from the computers of amateur rather than professional historians and offer few historiographic innovations. But while such digital history-whether created for the web or not-rarely departs from historiographic conventions, it vastly expands the traditionally limited audience for historical presentations and sometimes offers features not possible in print.

Online museum exhibits, for example, transcend the barriers of time (most exhibits are temporary installations), distance (museum visitors must be area residents or tourists), and space (gallery space is a scarce resource) that have often frustrated museum curators. Physical exhibits also translate naturally to the web because of their combination of text and images. But even that ambitious nationwide tour left most people unable to see the exhibit. Through the web, anyone with a computer can visit the full exhibit, although not share the experience of seeing the original painting.

Virtually every scholar who writes an article or book assembles an archive of sorts. Previously they could not readily share that archive given the expense of print publications. But web-based versions of journals have begun to offer supplements of primary sources. For example, Robert Darnton's 1999 presidential address to the American Historical Association on news and the media in eighteenth-century Paris, the first article with an electronic supplement published by the American Historical Review, includes a map of Paris, links to police reports, illustrations, and even songs.

The emerging experiments in electronic book publication such as the Gutenberg-e project sponsored by the American Historical Association and Columbia University Press, and the American Council of Learned Societies History e-book project, have also followed this practice. For example, Michael Katten's e-book Colonial Lists/Indian Power: Identity Formation in Nineteenth-Century Telugu-Speaking India includes photographs, sketches, maps, petitions, manuscripts, videos, statues, and palm leaf verses.

Web-based commercial history writing has generally not taken such an experimental approach and has moved from print to screen with few changes. The online articles at HistoryNet: Where History Lives on the Web-the offshoot of such popular history magazines as Civil War Times and Aviation History-are actually less interesting than the print originals. The web versions display mostly text and eschew the lavish illustrations of the print magazines-presumably to avoid the expense of picture permissions.

Enthusiasts and amateurs have put the greatest

energy into posting new forms of secondary literature online. Unlike the professional scholars and commercial popularizers, these amateurs traditionally have not had access to the print medium. They do not see the web as merely a new way to disseminate what has long been offered in print. Rather, it represents in many cases their first opportunity to be published. Thus, the web features a new genre of popular history writing that previously only had limited representation on library shelves-the passionate commentaries of people with a deep personal, but not professional, commitment to a historical topic.

Scholarly, public, and popular historians who have gone online have repeatedly confirmed the Library of Congress's early discovery that the web reaches unprecedented numbers of K-12 students and teachers. As a result, a very large percentage of websites, regardless of their primary focus, have incorporated teaching materials and advice. Although traditionally archives and libraries have eschewed a direct teaching function, on the web they have often embraced it.

American Memory's Learning Page offers many resources for teachers, including lesson plans, tips on searching the collections, and links to other websites. The National Archive and Record Administration's Digital Classroom offers a similar array of resources. Online lesson plans have become so ubiquitous that no one has yet cataloged them. Many museum sites offer extensive teaching resources.

While teaching enters at some level into many archival, museum, and even scholarly websites, a large number of sites put teaching and learning front and center. The most ubiquitous and numerous of these are syllabi-surely the most common history websites. Perhaps 30,000 history syllabi are posted on the web, with about half of those gated behind passwords through university sites and commercial courseware like WebCT and Blackboard.

Most online syllabi reduce logistic hassles common to college courses, such as needing to continually hand out lost assignments. Some, however, aim much higher. The online syllabus for Stanley Schultz's University of Wisconsin telecourse on the United States since the Civil War includes lecture notes, biographical sketches, exams and review sheets, a photographic gallery, and a directory of history websites. The website not only provides a syllabus and an extensive collection of primary sources (including books, posters, images, and early movies) but also a mystery about turn-of-the-century identity that students are asked to solve.

Along the way, it expresses an original historical thesis in non-narrative, multimedia terms. Course websites are almost always individual efforts. As a result, they reflect a personal vision, even one that is embodied only in the structure of course assignments, owing to limited design skills and time constraints. Particularly energetic and creative instructors like O'Malley, however, transcend these obstacles. The most extensive teaching sites generally reflect the efforts of a group or institution and external funding support from an agency like NEH, which has supported a number of online teaching projects.

Some of these large-scale projects have developed portals or resource centers for teachers in particular areas. For example, historians Thomas Dublin and Kathryn Kish Sklar at Binghamton University have, with support from NEH, created Women and Social Movements in the United States, 1775-2000. The site contains more than forty mini-monographs designed to be used in teaching; each one poses an interpretive question and offers a set of primary documents related to that question.

Similarly, Teacher Serve at the National Humanities Center offers extensive online materials for teaching about religion and the environment in American history. Still other projects strive to offer resource centers for even broader swaths of history. History Matters: The U.S. Survey Course on the Web, developed by CHNM in collaboration with the American Social History Project (ASHP) at the CUNY Graduate Center, presents a range of materials for teachers of U.S. history, including 1,000 primary documents in text, image, and audio; an annotated guide to more than 800 websites; model teaching assignments; sample syllabi; and moderated discussions about teaching with leading scholars.

A companion site, World History Matters, makes available some similar materials across an even broader canvas. Both sites also seek to give students the skills and tools needed to analyze the enormous number of primary sources that have become available online. As Randy Bass has pointed out, the web has put the "novice in the archive," but it has not taught him or her what to do there. Thus, History Matters and World History Matters provide guides and interactive exercises showing students how "expert learners" make sense of primary source evidence like films, music, maps, and traveler's accounts and to demonstrate how historical insights are formed.

9

Learning and Instruction Delivery

Most discussions of computers in education look at how new technologies might improve "instruction delivery," a management theorist's way of saying how teachers teach and how learners learn. Therefore, as resources for higher education continue to dwindle, when most people think of information technologies, it will usually be in terms of how such technologies might reduce the number of teachers needed or cut the time it takes learners to acquire skills. Some technologies do indeed help improve productivity in these ways.

Current successes are subject to several qualifications. Some cost savings are modest, others come with hidden prices, and all depend on careful attention to implementation in the classroom. But, although the data are still unclear, the economic logic behind the view is relatively straightforward: Cut costs by doing more with less; that is, hold student outcomes roughly constant while displacing labour (staff) with capital. With technology costs continually dropping while labour costs only rise, this trade-off appears a good one for increasing productivity.

Computer-aided Instruction and Computer-based Training

Computer-aided instruction (CAI) and computer-based

training (CBT) have shown some ability to do more with less, by providing learners drill-and-practice systems that replace teachers in routine coaching tasks. These systems are most frequently found in secondary schools but also play a role in remedial math, science, and language courses at the collegiate level, as well as in business and military training. However, as convenient as they might be for self-paced learning, CBT programmes often do not yield dramatic cost savings.

Development costs for multimedia courseware are usually very high, often offsetting savings in delivery, and the price of a stand-alone computer system for each student is sometimes so dear that labour costs must fall dramatically before any net savings appears. The latter situation may change in the future, however, as powerful machines drop roughly to the cost of a top-of-the-line TV.

Distance Learning

A few intelligent tutoring systems (ITS) also have reported cost-reductions in training. But, as with CAI and CBT, development costs currently impose strong limits on their productivity gains. In fact, the main attraction of ITS is that they may improve the quality of learning rather than reduce costs, as we discuss later under "Increasing Quality and Productivity." Today, distance learning—whereby students and teachers rely on electronic and hardcopy media, rather than on face-to-face contact, for at least some of their communication—provides probably the best examples of cost savings that are at least partly attributable to information technologies.

Several studies show that distance-learning courses in Asia cost from 45 to 90 percent of the cost of conventional college classes, with comparable student performance; costs can drop to as little as 8 percent of on-campus courses, although completion rates then also seem to dip. Using telecommunications to offer distance learning for over three decades, the Open University in Great Britain—one of the first very large-scale experiments in distance learning at the higher-education level—boasts average per-student costs of around one-half those of conventional campuses.

Open University: An Example in Achieving Cost Reductions. First, the technology must allow many students to be taught at once. Class sizes at the Open University usually exceed 200. The larger the class size, the greater the student-teacher ratio, which lowers labour costs and spreads high development and initial technology costs, leading, in turn, to productivity improvements. Break-even points—class sizes for which the cost of distance education and traditional delivery are roughly equal—will vary depending on, among other things, the size of technology investment and the course being taught.

But it is a safe bet, at least for the near term, that distance-learning classes of less than 20 will rarely lead to substantial per-student cost reductions. Second, a substantial amount of labour must be displaced by technology. Typically, labour is over 95 percent the cost of the class; so, modest trades of faculty for machines will not substantially change overall prices. Consequently, distance learning works best in relatively "standard" courses—math and the sciences—for which knowledge is relatively routine, can be embedded in the technology, and can have much teaching delegated to it.

Alternatively, to expand the range of courses that can be taught at a distance, the use of technology should be carefully designed so that expensive labour at least can be replaced by cheaper help. For example, the Open University makes liberal use of tutors, either in person or on the phone. Third, technology should substitute for labour as simply as possible. As the example of the Open University suggests, most low-cost distance learning does not fundamentally change the learning experience for the student, or the teacher. A computer application that promised to play a substantial role in teaching but that also demanded broad changes in faculty skills and activities could actually increase labour costs, even while guaranteeing a savings in teacher time.

The bottom line, then, is that today's distance-learning technology is largely limited to imparting relatively routine skills and knowledge, taught en masse, through relatively traditional methods. Most of the best examples actually come from military and corporate training, rather than from higher education. For example, large companies such as Ford now contract for distance instruction to help their employees learn how to use tools such as spreadsheets and word processors, as well as specialised equipment. And Hewlett-Packard estimates that it saves millions of dollars each year using distance learning to train employees more effectively and more efficiently than with conventional methods.

These examples explain why well over one-half of distance learning now goes on not in academic settings but in businesses—a market that is expanding so rapidly that whole TV networks are now dedicated to corporate distance learning. The Internet is increasingly being viewed as a medium that can bring distance learning and its cost benefits into the higher-education sector.

Internet Impact

At least partly to cut costs, almost all higher-education institutions in the United States are considering distance-learning programmes, dozens already have substantial offerings in place, and many universities are now moving in this direction. In the future, the Internet will be the most cost-effective way to deliver a new generation of distance-learning courses. By winter 1996, the U.S. Distance Learning Association listed many dozens of universities with homepages outlining their WWW and Internet-based courseware.

At the same time, the World Lecture Hall, a Web site managed by the University of Texas, has become a "virtual repository," organising links to hundreds of other sites that are making Web-based class materials available to anyone who is interested. Because the WWW first came online only in 1991, all these courses are new, and there are no solid data proving the effectiveness of Internet-based distance education. But a chemistry curriculum drawn almost at random from the World Lecture Hall illustrates some of the reasons why Web-based distance learning seems very promising, at least "on paper."

To begin with, emerging Internet courses can include a wealth of material about the class (lectures, exams, assignments) and references to relevant online literature (books, programmes, tools such as the periodic table), all accessible at the click of a mouse on a hypertext link. Each of these sources can be constructed as multimedia documents, including pictures, digitised audio versions of lectures, presentation overheads—even simulations, which can be run to give a much more dynamic impression of processes and structures.

Full high-bandwidth interactivity will be available soon, to support multi-person, multimedia dialogues in real-time. The new generation of Internet-based distance-learning courses, in short, can mix the graphics and video of instructional TV with a much more intimate style of interactive mentoring than teleconferencing ever could. Therefore, it should provide substantially richer learning experiences for students than the current generation does.

Web-based distance learning might enhance productivity in higher education in several ways. Most obviously, by providing a more powerful and flexible medium, the Web should enable developers to construct higher-quality courseware for a wider range of classes than ever before. With richer courseware, classes for which computers once replaced only a modest amount of labour might shortly be taught almost exclusively through technology; and in courses in which information technology previously had no part, it may play at least a supporting role. All this means that Web-based learning tools, appropriately used, promise to replace more labour and, consequently, to lower faculty costs.

Costs are dropping for several reasons:

— Hardware needed for Internet access is dropping quickly in price. In 1995 Web access required at least a low-end PC; less than two years later, "Internet appliances" such as WebTV permit Web surfing at about the cost of a television plus monthly cable charges.

— Network costs are dropping to zero. Or, more precisely, the cost of using the Internet is low and independent of distance, so it should be just as cheap to access distance-learning material from New Zealand as from next door. (This is why more and more people are using the Internet for their telephone service, to the consternation of long-distance phone companies.)

— De facto standards are making it easier to develop sharable courseware. The WWW is rooted in a few document and communication protocols to which most homepage builders currently adhere to. This may not make it easier to build any single distance-learning product, but, in the long run, it will help the community as a whole create better courseware.

But less-visible features of Internet-based distance learning—costs and standards—may enhance productivity even more dramatically. It is reasonable to assume that if courseware built on the Web is richer than previous distance-learning products, it might also be more costly to deliver—reasonable, but probably wrong. Although few realise it, the Internet is not only a better medium for learning and interaction but a cheaper way to deliver instruction—something providers of corporate training have already figured out.

For example, corporate providers are quickly trading their old on-demand video systems for more-flexible and less-expensive high-capacity intranets, which use Internet-style communication on private networks to deliver full-motion video to hundreds of viewers at once, at the click of a mouse. Schools and homes can expect similar benefits, even if they cannot afford the high-capacity LANs of big business. High-bandwidth yet low-cost connections to the WWW will soon come in several forms.

Many homes today can access the Internet cheaply through ISDN phone connections, providing about 5 to 10 times the effective bandwidth of ordinary phone lines. More interestingly, successful trials of cable modems in 1996 promise very high-speed Internet connections, at roughly the cost of standard cable service. If this promise is realised, the much-heralded-but-never-accomplished "500 channels of cable TV" finally could turn into something really useful. And, because they require no new and costly infrastructure development, wireless connections, such as DirectPC, may be the most promising of all.

In short, the technical problems facing the installation of inexpensive wide-bandwidth Internet connections are all but solved; the policy barriers, however, loom large.

In addition to reducing educational costs, the shrinking price of delivering Internet-based distance learning should help address other challenges for higher education. For one thing, Internet-based distance learning could be conveniently accessible to many different kinds of learners. Part of this improved access simply means putting more people in touch with more learning resources. A new wave of cheap "Internet appliances" should bring Internet access within almost anyone's budget; anyone who can afford Nintendo should be able to afford the WWW.

And once on the Internet, all resources are equally inexpensive to browse, whether they happen to be on a homepage next door or thousands of miles away. Equally important for improved access is the ability of Internet distance learning to reach consumers at any place and any time. This flexibility will be especially important, for example, to workers who want to "retool" skills at night while working during the day.

At the broadest level, an Internet style of learning or instruction delivery will, we believe, be so common that it makes little sense to view distance learning as a special form of education delivery. Since Internet and Web tools will continue to drop in cost and increase in functionality for the foreseeable future, technology should, over time, displace more and more faculty labour. Further, what labour cannot be displaced will at least not have to be nearby: The Internet can connect students with faculty and peers as easily as it connects learners with multimedia documents.

Eventually, then, most learning will be distance-independent, and the special cases will be those that are geographically bound. Perhaps more to the point, distance learning should be viewed as a common tool in higher education, not as a separate—and esoteric—option. And most courses should be designed to use distance learning in some capacity, and often in a variety of capacities. A wide range of experiments in distance learning are already under way, and they come in many forms, rather than all fitting one mold.

The degree to which direct interactions are replaced can vary significantly: Telecommunications are sometimes little more than an add-on to classroom lectures; conversely, taped lectures may be the centerpiece of instruction, with face-to-face tutoring serving as a supplement; in still other cases, all discussion happens at a distance. There is no single, obvious way to order courses from light to heavy users of distance-learning technology. Some courses that are, for example, offered exclusively at a distance still make less use of telecommunication connections than classes that also include some direct contact. We ordered the following list roughly from courses that provide narrow connectivity, overall, to those that provide rich interactions.

Early distance-learning courses through postal mail trafficked only in text, and a single interchange required days, if not weeks—not at all interactive by today's standards. Videotaped lectures distributed from a centralised source offer much greater bandwidth but no more interactivity; on the other hand, e-mail discussions between teachers and students are highly interactive but narrow in bandwidth. Some of the newest Internet-based distance learning enjoys both broadband, multimedia connections and real-time interactions, often linking not only faculty with students, but students with one another and with shared online resources.

While earlier distance-learning models delivered knowledge from a centralised teacher to students through narrow, slow, and separate connections, newer models look much more like an electronic community, tying together students, faculty, and distributed tools in a rich, speedy web of digital contacts. With so many variants, it is no surprise that what makes an application of information technology an instance of distance learning is becoming less and less clear.

For example, courseware such as the chemistry curriculum in the World Lecture Hall might be used in a distance-learning class; but right now, it is simply online material for an on-campus course. However, merely by skipping lectures and labs and relying on the rich Web documents to compensate for reduced in-person contact, individual students may turn it into a virtual distance-learning course. Such individual experiments, which probably have gone on informally for decades, now are leading to large-scale studies that will try to gauge the importance of distance as a barrier to learning in technology-intensive courses.

It is useful to view this increasing freedom from spatial location in terms of the progressive "unbundling" of teaching functions in higher education as educational technologies have changed across time. Centuries ago, when knowledge was conveyed exclusively through an oral tradition, location was everything. With the advent of written texts, students were freed from the need to attend lectures; however, other important functions, including tutoring, counseling, and evaluation, remained essentially face-to-face activities. Now, just as books have weakened the links between distance and learning in the past, today new information technologies can almost break them. Since the Internet can connect students with teachers as easily as it connects students with course material, tutoring and counseling can be done through e-mail and real-time chat rooms.

Similarly, as reference materials increasingly become available in digital form, students will no longer need proximity to libraries. Evaluation and assessment also can be done at a distance. Written products, such as essays, already are created routinely with word processors; sending them across a network for grading can be easier than printing them and walking them into a professor's office. Multiple-choice as well as short-answer tests have been computerised for years.

Again, the point is not that learning should be conducted at a distance, just that creative applications make distance less and less of a barrier to learning. The challenge will be to discover the most effective applications of distance-learning technology and to blend them together with traditional face-to-face transactions.

Increasing Quality and Productivity

While many applications of information technology in education try to reduce costs, others focus on the output side of the productivity equation: helping students learn more or better, or to learn new skills—applications rarely included in higher-education curricula. A collection of examples illustrates several ways in which information-technology applications could lead to better learning and teaching outcomes.

Most successful computer-aided instruction and computer-based training applications boast of cost reductions, but a few also claim gains in the quality of student learning. Some of these applications rely on distinctly cutting-edge technology, making lavish use of multimedia, and engaging students in highly interactive discussions. However, other ideas are surprisingly simple. For example, The Teaching Company (TTC) thinks that the videotapes and audiotapes it offers can help college students improve grades in everything from history to psychology to physics.

Of course, these tapes lack the interactivity of a good tutoring session, but TTC is gambling that the quality of its tapes will more than compensate: The lectures are delivered by elite, "superstar" faculty in each field, not by merely competent professors. Some very positive reviews of these products may be too optimistic. However, in the future, Web technology could clearly make educational packages featuring superstar instructors easier to develop and more broadly accessible, perhaps leading to significant improvements in teaching and learning productivity.

Imagine, for example, a course built around master lectures, digitised and put online, and combined with complementary assignments, projects, tutorials, and group discussions—like those already found in World Lecture Hall courses. Taking this course through the Internet might not be quite the same as being there in person, which would require being a student at MIT, Stanford, or a similarly elite and pricey institution. Nonetheless, for less-fortunate students, such an online course could be better than an in-person course offered by a second-tier university. Here, as in other areas, information technology might lead to improvements in productivity by making truly great—not merely competent—practitioners and their performances available to almost everyone.

Intelligent Tutoring Systems

While replicating outstanding teaching performances on video might lead to improvements in learning productivity, a much more ambitious approach is to try to capture, in software, the reasoning of teachers. Of course, this cannot be done just by pointing a camera at a smart talking head. Rather, the process of developing so-called intelligent tutoring systems (ITS) begins with an expert system—a collection of heuristic rules—that is capable of answering questions and solving problems in a given subject matter.

For instance, the expert system inside a good calculus ITS would be able to solve arbitrary symbolic integration problems, and would do so in a way that approximates how an "ideal" human mathematician would reason. The expert system in an ITS is often supplemented with a student-modeling capability, which can examine a student's reasoning, find the exact step at which he or she went astray, try to diagnose the reasons for the error, and even suggest ways of overcoming the impasse. The potential value of such highly intelligent systems is obvious.

Indeed, for decades, the idea of supplying students with their own automated tutor, capable of tailoring learning experiences to students' needs at a fine level, has been the holy grail of teaching technology—with good reason. Many studies have shown that one-on-one tutoring is the best way to learn. And for a few academic subjects, ITS have nearly matched the capabilities of their human-tutor counterparts, helping to raise students' scores one letter grade or more. However, while such systems show that ITS can raise the output side of the productivity equation in education, their successes to date are very limited. Because they try to embed detailed human-reasoning skills, both in subject-matter areas and in teaching expertise, they rely on advances in cognitive theory and software engineering.

But these disciplines have yielded a detailed understanding of thinking in only a very few well-defined subjects; consequently, ITS currently are confined to relatively simple parts of algebra, geometry, computer programming, physics, and other sciences. In higher education, then, ITS probably would be most appropriate in basic freshman and remedial classes. And, needless to say, even in these subjects, automated tutors come nowhere near the ability to mimic superstar teachers. On the contrary, ITS are frequently called "brain damaged" by most computer scientists, their developers included. Over time, however, ITS will get smarter and smarter.

Buttressed by advances in cognitive science, they will capture an increasing share of human-teaching expertise, and they will extend to a wider range of subjects. However, all evidence suggests progress here will be slow. While the speed of computer hardware continues roughly to double every two years, the intelligence of computer software, however you measure it, creeps ahead at a snail's pace. But this does not mean that information technology is destined to play only a minor role in helping improve the quantity and quality of learning in higher education. It just means that some of the most obvious ways in which technology attempts to partially replace faculty as lecturers or tutors in a traditional classroom setting may not be the most promising ways, at least in the short run.

Interactive Learning Environments

Some of the most successful applications of information technology follow a very different principle: Instead of mimicking human tutors, they provide rich, simulated environments that enable students or trainees to practice skills intensively. Flight simulators, the first such learning environments, are still perhaps the most compelling ones. For decades they have been singularly effective technologies for improving the quality of pilot training. In the protective environment of a virtual cockpit, pilots can perfect difficult maneuvers, trying them over and over without fear of the deadly effects of a real-world mistake.

SHERLOCK, a descendent in spirit of these early simulators, demonstrates similarly impressive outcomes: Students can learn electronics troubleshooting and fault-diagnosis skills in less than one-tenth the time they previously required. While SHERLOCK includes some important coaching supports, the basic reason that trainees acquire skills so rapidly is simply that the system can present students with simulated problem situations that arise only rarely in the real world—namely, troubleshooting the complex hardware that diagnoses faulty F-15 avionics.

Trainees do not learn these troubleshooting skills very quickly in the field, because problems that might foster new knowledge naturally occur, say, once every few weeks. Using SHERLOCK, such problems can be made to order every few minutes, if necessary. More generally, this and other virtual worlds rely on the fact that one of the most powerful ways to learn is by doing; but learning-by-doing works well only if the world cooperates by providing the learner with a large number of practice cases, and cases suitable to the learner's current level of expertise. In situations where the real world cannot be easily controlled or does not readily cooperate, computers can now provide rich simulated worlds, at an arbitrarily high degree of fidelity, that can be controlled with the click of a mouse.

In theory, just as SHERLOCK provides trainees with a large number of rich avionics cases, these simulations might present learners with, say, a series of hypothetical history scenarios, some of which may have analogs in real historical events and some not. These technologies appear very interesting, but they are also very new. Whether they can lead to the dramatic gains in the quantity of learning we find with SHERLOCK remains to be seen.

Some of the applications that promise to help raise educational productivity by improving student learning, rather than by cutting costs, are already network-based systems. In CoVis, for example, students use the Internet to communicate with distant mentors, collaborate on projects with peers, gather data from remote sites, and talk with experts in atmospheric and environmental sciences. But many of the cutting-edge applications are stand-alone systems that run on only one or a few computer platforms. For instance, one might work on a Macintosh but not on a PC. Even worse, since many of these systems are still research prototypes, they may run on only relatively high-end machines.

All this would seem to mean that some of the most interesting new information technologies for higher education will be, for the foreseeable future, either inaccessible to most students or prohibitively expensive for schools or students to acquire. Not necessarily. One way around this problem, again, exploits the Internet and the WWW. It is already possible for stand-alone software systems to piggyback on the near-standard protocols for creating WWW documents.

In doing so, these systems can be made available very widely and relatively cheaply. As anyone who uses the WWW knows, Web browsers and servers, unlike most software, run on a wide range of machines. The considerable complexities of making key languages and protocols de facto standards are hidden from the average user, who can happily create documents that will appear on any machine just about the same as they look on his or hers. Technically, only WWW documents enjoy this relative machine independence. However, using scripting languages that enable programmes to be initiated on remote machines and new homepages to be created and loaded on the fly, it is possible to turn almost any piece of educational software into a distance-learning application.

The cleverness needed to turn isolated software into sharable distance-learning systems on the WWW might be of technical interest to some readers. But such technical subtleties miss the key point of the example: Already, the Internet and WWW permit high-powered applications that run only on high-powered machines to be accessed by students who might have available only low-end machines—and almost any kind of low-end machine, not just those that the original application developer envisioned. The future looks even more promising, on several scores.

First, as already noted, ultra-cheap Internet appliances should bring down access cost even further. Second, the protocols needed to make products widely sharable across the Internet, using almost any hardware platform, are quickly falling into place. Tricks now required to turn the WWW into an interactive medium will soon lose their appeal, primarily because new Web tools, and languages such as Java, for building "live computational objects", will soon provide primitives that make this kind of interactivity easy to achieve rather than a challenging problem to solve. All this may mean that higher education can have its cake and eat it too.

Most of the current cutting-edge information-technology applications we reviewed promise to help students learn better or faster, or both. Improving educational productivity in this sense is clearly an important goal for higher education. But, until recently, this goal seemed at odds with others: reducing the cost of delivering education and increasing access to education by an increasingly diverse population of students. Without question, in the future, most applications of technology in education that offer exciting possibilities for transforming teaching and learning will continue to be developed in corporate and university research settings on high-end machines.

And these will probably remain expensive, well beyond the means of almost all students and even most higher-education departments and computer labs. However, high-bandwidth networks, coupled with increasingly standardised software languages and communication protocols, and with ever-cheaper Internet terminals, should bring these cutting-edge applications within reach of learners and teachers who do not have access to the newest and fastest technologies. This does not mean that poor students will enjoy all the same access to technology-based learning as wealthy ones, of course. There will always be computers that offer more functionality at a higher price.

And even if high-quality educational materials could be accessed by anyone on any machine at any time, nothing right now prevents providers from metering this access and charging whatever the market will bear. The point, however, is that information technology by itself will no longer be a significant barrier to access; if anything, the WWW and Internet should be a force toward greater access to and equity in education.

Many Interesting Options, Many Hard Choices

Certainly information technologies do more than provide better tools with which to deliver instruction and learning materials in higher education, but such tools still dominate the field of educational technology. First, it should be obvious that information technologies offer many different ways to improve instruction delivery, not just one. Looking just at distance learning, there is a rich set of options to choose from.

Selecting from the different choices demands attention to the educational goals the technologies address. Some might help higher-education institutions reduce costs; others look better-suited to increasing access to educational resources, or to increasing the quantity, quality, or speed of student learning. Overall, the proliferation of Internet and WWW resources should steadily bring down the cost of all educational software products and services. Yet, some will be more costly than others, and a few will still be very expensive for the foreseeable future.

In general, then, it is a mistake to assume that information technology provides one or a few ways to improve learning and teaching, and it is equally wrong to believe that technology applications will affect just a single educational goal: cost reduction. A third assumption, probably more widely believed, is also wrong: that information technology is mainly a vehicle to enhance educational productivity. While some, such as SHERLOCK, clearly intend to help speed up learning, or to improve learning of well-defined subject areas, it is much less obvious how others are trying to improve educational productivity in any simple sense.

Instead, they are generally trying to transform the processes and products of learning. For example, they might exploit new visualisation technologies to enable junior students to learn about complex systems that previously only graduate students found comprehensible; and they might foster deeper understanding through inquiry-based learning rather than traditional lectures, or through collaborative-learning methods that simply never existed prior to high-bandwidth networks.

In short, here information technology is a driver of educational reform, not of productivity enhancement unless productivity is redefined to include a wide range of qualitative changes, not just quantitative improvements. That these applications transform processes and products of learning more than they enhance productivity has several implications for their adoption, implementation, and costs. Consider, from the point of view of the developer, how many different facets of an educational context might need to change for the potentially impressive benefits of such applications to be realised.

Clearly, the technology itself—the tools actually used by students in learning—is just the tip of the iceberg. Other possible changes range from the roles of teachers, to methods of evaluating learning, to deeper philosophical views of how learning happens and what constitutes knowledge.

10

Library Support for Online Learners

The Internet, has posed new challenges for library services. E-learners and traditional learners now have access to a universe of digital information through the information superhighway. New information and communications technologies, as well as new educational models, require librarians to re-evaluate the way they develop, manage and deliver resources and services.

Historically, librarians have sought to provide services to distance learners that are equivalent to those available to on-campus learners, and this aspiration is grounded in the philosophical frameworks of the Canadian Library Association's Guidelines for Library Support of Distance and Distributed Learning in Canada and the Association of College and Research Libraries' Guidelines for Distance Learning Library Services. Both the Canadian and the American Guidelines recognise that distance learners frequently do not have direct access to the full range of library services and materials, and that in this situation, the goal of equity makes it necessary that librarians services that are more "personalised" than might be expected on campus.

The library literature provides a rich record of service models and best practices, and there has been an explosion in publication as librarians consider ways to support learners in a networked environment. What do e-learners need from librarians? Suggestions advocating change in librarians' roles in support of distance learning in the information age appear throughout the literature: librarians "must assert themselves as key players in the learning process thereby changing their roles from information providers to educators" ; they have become providers of technical support; and they have been transformed from "information gatekeepers" to "information gateways".

In responding to the need to provide ongoing online library support, librarians have worked at translating what they do in a traditional library into virtual or digital environments, while customising their services and resources for e-learners. Traditionally, libraries offer circulation services, interlibrary loans, course reserves, an information desk, a reference desk, and library instruction. To serve learners connected to their institutional library primarily through a computer network, librarians are providing remote access to, and electronic delivery of, library resources, and are using communication technologies to deliver electronic reference services and instructional support. When we speak of providing support to e-learners, we are referring to a wider community of learners than the term "student" suggests.

An academic library's learners may include students, faculty, staff, researchers, and so on. The library is seen as a source of training and guidance to a community of learners who are concerned with navigating the complexities of locating and using digital resources and services. Moreover, the move toward an online environment has resulted in a shift from the systematic oneto-one information flow of the past to a new model in which the users and the providers of information are able to relate in a manyto-many, dynamic relationship.

For example, in the traditional model, a librarian provides a bridge between learners and information providers by selecting and cataloguing resources and by providing assistance with these resources. In the new model, the library serves as a facilitator by offering ongoing support enabling learners to interact and exchange knowledge with others, to communicate directly with the publishers and vendors of information resources, and to participate in a collaborative endeavor to make available rich collections of online scholarly information resources.

The virtual library is the concept of remote access to the contents and services of libraries and other information resources, combining an on-site collection of current and heavily used materials in both print and electronic form, with an electronic network which provides access to, and delivery from, external worldwide library and commercial information and knowledge sources.

Additional terms for the virtual library include the "digital library," the "electronic library," and the "library without walls." Many libraries are hybrids, providing virtual access to electronic resources and services, while maintaining and supporting use of a physical collection housed in a library building. With the tremendous growth of the Internet, e-learners have access to an overwhelming range of information sources available at the click of a mouse: library resources; government information; news sites; advertising; even whole Web sites devoted to Elvis sightings, crop circles, and JFK conspiracy theories.

Librarians have traditionally selected and organised resources with great care. In building virtual libraries, librarians have the opportunity to provide e-learners with direction and to rescue them from information overload. A virtual library can link e-learners to library catalogues, licensed journal databases, electronic book collections, selected Internet resources, electronic course reserves, and tutorials, and to forums for communication and interaction with librarians. The virtual library permits e-learners to access library and networked resources and services anytime and anywhere that an Internet connection and computing equipment are available.

Library Resources

Technology offers opportunities to be innovative but it is important to bear in mind that not all e-learners are equal when it comes to access to computing equipment; the availability, speed, and stability of Internet connections; or the information skills that are needed to make optimum use of virtual libraries. Access to print-based library materials continues to be important, because not all of the information resources that elearners need are available in electronic format: many of our most valuable research materials are still print-based. The Digital Library Federation and the Council on Library and Information Resources commissioned a survey of the use of print and electronic scholarly information resources at institutions of higher education across the United States.

The survey found that, although almost half of undergraduates report using electronic resources all or most of the time for their coursework, this was the case for only 35.2% of graduate students. Only 34.7% of faculty indicated that they use electronic resources all or most of the time for their research, and just 22.7% said this of their teaching. Although there has been a shift away from purchasing print materials to be housed in a physical building and toward providing access to licensed digital resources made available over a computer network, librarians continue to work to resolve issues pertaining to distance delivery of resources that are unavailable in digital format.

Online catalogues and indexing and abstracting systems provide elearners with convenient access to bibliographic information about valuable scholarly documents. When those documents are not available in full-text form online, a demand is generated for delivery from a library's print collection or from the collections of other libraries through interlibrary loans. Typical solutions for delivery of non-digital formats include the use of mail and courier services, the establishment of collections at designated sites, and the negotiation of agreements with other libraries through consortia.

Given that a growing number of learners are accessing library collections online, librarians are working to develop an integrated approach to providing access to electronic resources that facilitates retrieval and reduces confusion. A library Web site can function as an information gateway, an entry point to a range of online resources, with key components being the library catalogue and journal databases. Most online catalogues permit the integration of electronic books and electronic journals, enabling learners to locate items from digital and physical collections with one search.

User services-such as the ability to check due dates, renew materials, and request materials online-are also provided. Gateways may also organise collections and incorporate directories like that provided by Athabasca University's Journal Databases: List Databases by Subject page. Librarians have become increasingly creative in enhancing their Web sites. Because not all e-learners have physical access to reference tools-the quick fact-finding tools that are the staple of library collections-libraries can perform a valuable service by providing pointers to online versions.

Athabasca University Library's Digital Reference Centre, for example, offers a digital version of an academic library's reference collection, including almanacs and directories, atlases and maps, data and statistics, and dictionaries and encyclopedias. Librarians select quality Internet resources to help e-learners navigate the Web. For example, the British Open University Library's ROUTES database contains quality-assessed, courserelated Internet resources "selected by course teams and the Library's Information Specialists".

As libraries work to enhance their presence on the Web, a growing number are investigating the potential of electronic course reserves (e-reserves). The traditional course reserves desk of an academic library, with its limited copies, short loan periods, and high late fines, can be a considerable source of frustration for students. In the e-reserves model, the library makes available, through the World Wide Web, items that faculty have selected and "placed on reserve" for students in a particular course. San Diego State University (SDSU) pioneered e-reserves in the early 1990s. SDSU uses Docutek's ERes, a system that provides access to course readings, chat rooms, and bulletin boards. Many other libraries have initiated their own projects.

Electronic delivery of course reserve material has become a hot topic in the library literature. The Association of Research Libraries (ARL) maintains the Electronic Reserves Listserv, and an archive of the discussion can be accessed on the Web. Most e-reserves operate on a password-protected model: one must be affiliated with the institution, or even registered in the course, to view course reserves. A typical e-reserve solution is to employ an electronic course reserve module that permits full integration with the library's online catalogue. Content in ereserves databases varies.

Scanning and mounting readings in portable document format (PDF) is time-consuming and requires copyright clearance. Other options for content include incorporating institution-produced materials (e.g., lecture notes and video or audio clips), using licensed digital resources through direct linking to items by means of a persistent URL, and including selected resources freely available through the World Wide Web. Librarians can take a creative, pro-active approach to e-reserves. Athabasca University Library has developed a platform for ereserves that operates on a somewhat different model than do other e-reserves systems.

The Digital Reading Room offers a digital solution for course readings and supplementary materials. An in-house storage and retrieval system was developed for the DRR using open source software. The model operates along the principle of open access to collection creation tools, thus permitting course content creators, educational media developers, and librarians to develop a multidisciplinary knowledge database. Each course in the Digital Reading Room has a Digital Reading File (DRF).

The licensed contents, such as journal database articles, require authentication through the Library's proxy server, permitting only the Athabasca University community of users to access them; non-licensed resources, such as Web sites, are freely available to the public. A search engine permits e-learners to search across the DRFs, providing a multidisciplinary aspect to course reserves that is not typically encountered. By encouraging the inclusion of resources in a variety of formats, including text, graphics, video, audio, simulations, and games, the DRR supports a wide range of learning objectives and styles.

The DRR accommodates the inclusion of non-digital resources by providing e-learners with a means to request them from the Library. The DRR is being developed using metatags that conform to the IEEE LOM standards and use the CanCore implementation guidelines to insure consistency and search capability across database collections such as MERLOT. Managing the remote access and authentication issues involved in making digital resources available has become a significant area of support to users of the electronic library. Librarians may be called upon to respond to questions concerning log-in and password information, browser configuration, software installation, and a range of troubleshooting needs.

Access problems are hugely frustrating for e-learners, and must be resolved quickly. Ensuring that front-line library staff are adequately trained, providing clear instructions on the library's Web site, and coordinating support activities with computing services personnel can contribute to effective technical support. E-learners also benefit from having a variety of means of contacting the library, including e-mail, Web forms, and a toll-free telephone number.

Challenges and Opportunities in Library Services

Reference

E-learners require more than access to e-resources. Traditionally, a reference librarian acts as an additional type of resource, one who can be counted upon to provide expertise in making sense of library systems and research tools, and to offer a helping hand along that often slippery path known as the research process. Virtual library users face additional challenges in mining relevant information out of a computer system that "obstinately" returns zero hits in response to a query that does not match the character strings in its database files.

The most common means of providing electronic reference services to remote users has been e-mail, the advantages and disadvantages of which have been well documented in the literature. The around-the-clock and around-the-world accessibility of e-mail allows users to connect with librarians beyond the walls of library buildings and outside the usual hours of operation. E-mail provides a written record of requests and responses, permits the electronic transmission of search results, and allows librarians time to reflect on requests. One of the most serious concerns about e-mail reference services is their impact on the traditional face-to-face reference interview, particularly the absence of the verbal and non-verbal cues that typically assist a librarian in effectively responding to a question.

Hulshof identifies three issues related to the use of electronic communication in serving virtual patrons (e-learners): immediacy, intricacy, and interaction. Because it is so easy for a learner to send a request electronically and have it arrive at the library instantly, there is a perception that the librarian's response will be as immediate. The learner may become frustrated, not realising that the process of locating information and developing a response takes the librarian just as long when the request is made electronically as when it is made in person or in any other way.

The more intricate or complex the request, the longer it will take for the librarian to clarify it and respond appropriately: a series of e-mail messages may be required, which will further reduce the immediacy of the e-mail request. Immediacy and intricacy relate to the lack of interaction: the opportunity to discuss and clarify inquiries that occurs in person or over the telephone is not so easily accommodated by e-mail. There are ways to deal with some of these issues.

A welldesigned reference Web form, such as that provided on the Ask AU Library: Ask about a Research

Topic Web page, which encourages elearners to include full identifying and course information, to describe clearly their research problem and search terminology, and to state the parameters of the assignment, can clarify requests for librarians and reduce the need to e-mail back and forth. Automated replies, which are sent out by the e-mail programme in response to the receipt of a message, can be used to reassure e-learners that their messages are being received, and can let them know what to expect in terms of service.

E-mail reference service can be enhanced and supplemented with additional technologies that raise the level of interaction with realtime or live communication. Chat technology allows e-learners and librarians to send text messages back and forth instantly, using a form of communication that is familiar to most Internet users. There have been a number of library experiments with Web contact center software, which is modeled on the private sector's online solution to providing customer support.

Web contact center software provides a higher level of interaction than does basic chat software, allowing for queuing and routing of messages, as well as enabling librarians to "push" Web pages to users. Providing e-learners with a toll-free telephone number remains an effective and convenient reference services strategy, particularly for intricate inquiries. The telephone reference interview works best when both librarian and e-learner are working in front of computers connected to the Internet.

E-learners are frequently silent and invisible as they search and explore a library's online resources, and they do not have the same access that on-campus learners have to formal library instruction sessions. With the array of digital resources available to them, the multiplicity of interfaces and search tools, and the need for evaluation and critical thinking when using the Internet for research, "information literacy" skills are a must-have for e-learners. Information literacy refers to competencies with information sources in a variety of formats. According to the Association of College and Research Libraries, an information literate individual is able to

— Determine the extent of information needed

— Access the needed information effectively and efficiently

— Evaluate information and its sources critically

— Incorporate selected information into one's knowledge base

— Use information effectively to accomplish a specific purpose

— Understand the economic, legal, and social issues surrounding the use of information, and access and use information ethically and legally

Supporting the integration of information literacy skills training into the core curriculum has become an important issue for libraries. As an extension of their traditional role of providing library instruction sessions and developing instructional materials, librarians are designing online tutorials and courses that promote information literacy and encourage active learning. Particularly fine examples are the University of Texas System Digital Library's TILT-Texas Information Literacy Tutorial; and Utah Academic Library Consortium's Internet Navigator, a multi-institutional online course developed by a team of librarians and Web developers.

The British Open University Library has developed SAFARI, a freely available interactive tutorial, as well as an information literacy course called MOSAIC (Making Sense of Information in the Connected Age). Many libraries provide instruction to e-learners by making information available on their Web pages, including frequently asked questions, library glossaries, research guides, and "how-to" pages. Athabasca University Library's Digital Reference Centre integrates resources with contextual instruction and provides links to instructional resources, including a detailed guide to Internet searching that encourages e-learners to think critically about Internet resources, and library research guides such as the AU Library Guide to Researching Topics in Women's Studies.

Online tutorials usually operate on a model in which the elearner interacts in isolation with a computer. Their effectiveness can be enhanced by the addition of more interactive forms of instruction. The librarians at the Florida Distance Learning Reference and Referral Center, for example, have experimented with chat software to simulate a virtual classroom and open up "live" group instruction to e-learners. Librarians can also work with faculty to develop a library thread in a course discussion area, or to open a discussion forum on the library Web pages.

In reviewing definitions of the virtual library, Sloan identifies an emphasis on the technological and informational building blocks, and a neglect of human components, such as the service tradition and human interaction. The continuing changes in technology have been truly astonishing, and the scope for building new information services and new ways of representing content seem unlimited. However, it is very important to remember that investment in human capital is also a strategic investment, especially when introducing new technologies, procedures, and processes. Although technology is the key infrastructure of the virtual library-a tool used to support library goals-human factors are the most important determinants of the success of the virtual library.

The digital library serves mainly as a facilitator in organising and providing knowledge and resources to its users. Sharing knowledge and information among library staff, researchers, faculty, students, and other departments within the institution encourages them to work together, develop their skills, and form strong and trusting relationships. A focus on collaboration between the library and the faculty promotes a responsive approach to course design and supports teaching and learning objectives, particularly when this collaboration incorporates student contributions and feedback.

All parties must have a common vision in which each one participates actively by contributing their skills and perspectives to the building of a genuine partnership. This new approach considers the library as an active partner of the learning community, helping learners to become "information literates" by integrating information literacy skills into the curriculum. For example, the library can help learners to evaluate critically the authority and authenticity of the resources they find, and to enhance their critical thinking skills. The library can also offer support to learners, and can mentor their work by offering one-to-one communication and interaction, and by achieving a deeper level of understanding of what learners need.

From a research perspective, a number of models can be involved in creating an environment that is responsive to the scholarly information needs of a diverse group of e-learners. Librarians locate, select and describe quality Internet resources, and provide access to journal databases and electronic book collections, providing e-learners with full-text content from a wide range of online resources and publications, including peer-reviewed journals. Within this framework, the library works with faculty, researchers, scholarly societies, and publishers in developing and managing a collection of enriched online scholarly resources.

Such a partnership enables researchers to interact with others, exchange experiences, and publish their works online. The library role is thus transformed from simply being a provider of library resources, into meeting the ongoing support needs of the parties involved. The library also serves to foster research skills by encouraging students and other learners to search, investigate, discover, and take advantage of these valuable online resources. Management support is as much a key to success in developing the virtual library as in any other project. Athabasca University's strategic plan incorporates a distinct section related to library strategies and projects, and explains how these strategies are aligned with the overall mission of the University.

A virtual library should have a high profile leader, a key person who can work to obtain the support of the institution's management and promote a climate of change. In addition, the leader must work with different groups within the institution to ensure that the project responds to their specific needs and goals. For example, when Athabasca University Library initiated the Digital Reading Room project as an enhanced electronic course reserves system, the Library entered into partnership with the Educational Media Development unit to ensure a best practices approach to Web- and visual-design aspects.

Consultation with faculty has been an ongoing element of the project, with faculty selecting content and acting as consultants in evaluating the design and functionality of the DRR in relation to their course development and delivery needs. All staff involved in providing library support to e-learners must be included in the partnership. Technological changes have been the dominant force reshaping library services. Instilling a culture of sharing, motivation, equity, and active partnering encourages library staff to respond positively to the changing roles, responsibilities, and skills that the integration and use of technology requires.

A well-designed, ongoing training programme enables library staff to upgrade their skills to their new assignments, and helps them to understand and control fear of change. External partnerships, collaborative efforts, and consortia form another important bridge to the effective support of e-learners. Within Canada, university libraries extend in-person borrowing privileges to students, faculty, and staff from across the country through the Canadian University Reciprocal Borrowing Agreement. There are also initiatives to share virtual reference desks, such as the National Library of Canada's Virtual Reference Canada, which allow learners to benefit from the range of information resources and staff expertise available at a variety of participating institutions.

Consortial approaches to database subscriptions enable libraries to expand the scope of the electronic resources they are able to offer their learners in a time of shrinking budgets and escalating journal costs. The Canadian National Site Licensing Project negotiates licensing agreements that permit participating universities across Canada to access a suite of research databases in the science, engineering, health and environmental disciplines.

11

External Providers of Education

The proprietary training sector covers a wide range of schools and providers. Some grant degrees; others offer only short courses and training seminars. Some focus on routine clerical, sales, and cosmetics skills; still others offer professional classes in law and architecture. About the only feature all share is that fees and tuition cover costs, since none is supported directly through taxes.

Because their operations are so different, it has been difficult to measure the size of this sector in relation to public and private academic institutions. Clearly, however, it is a large and growing sector. California alone now boasts thousands of proprietary schools, bringing in an estimated $1.4 billion in tuition as of 1992. This sector promises to expand substantially because, in the future, businesses (not individuals) will be the primary clients. In 1994, businesses spent roughly $50 billion on training. Whereas much of that training was done in-house in the past, it is increasingly being outsourced to external providers.

Probably the biggest, and certainly the fastest-expanding, part of this sector belongs to companies providing training in using new information technologies.

In 1995, corporations in the United States paid over $15 billion in information-technology training, a figure that will probably grow about 15 percent per year to over $30 billion by the end of the century. Such courses cover everything from mastering the nuances of Windows 95 to acquiring much more generic skills in object-oriented programming, analysis, and design.

Not surprisingly, the courses are not only about high technology but use that technology, originating, generally, with external providers who specialise in training products that make the heaviest, and often most innovative, uses of information technology. The Teaching Company and Learning Tree offer thousands of computer-based training (CBT) course products, most created to meet the needs of large corporate clients. Microsoft, Intel, Novell, and other large software and hardware companies also offer a wide range of training courses. But theirs are courses tailored primarily to their own products, rather than to clients' interests.

In some respects aiming at one-stop shopping for training, it supplies online enrollment, certification programmes, exam preparation, and a list of Web-based courses. But MOLI's relationship with students, course providers, and specific classes is actually anything but traditional. More like GNA than Athena, MOLI mainly furnishes the infrastructure and value-added services that organise Web-based courses on such products as Visual Basic, C++, and Word.

Third-party online content vendors (OCVs) develop most of the interactive courseware products; different groups, called authorised online classroom providers (OCPs), build specific classes from these materials, adding human learning advisors and other curriculum material as needed. Students then interact with MOLI by searching the course-list database to find OCPs whose courses meet their needs and whose location is suitable.

Students also can make use of various common information resources in MOLI, such as the student union, library, advising center, and bookstore. Just as it provides various tools to help consumers, MOLI also attends very carefully to its suppliers. In contrast to the World Lecture Hall, which seems to accept all course offerings it receives, MOLI constrains course providers in at least three ways. First, the Institute defines the topics for which it will accept courseware. Second, it evaluates courseware and classes, and admits only those OCVs and OCPs that it authorises.

Third, it imposes standards for courseware development that help ensure that Web-based content developed by different OCVs will run on a wide range of platforms and will work well when put together into larger course products. MOLI encourages content vendors and course providers to meet these demands by offering tools and infrastructure, including the bookstore and library, that help create high-quality products.

But the primary incentive is financial: OCVs can sell curricula to OCPs and to other interested (but not authorised) parties through the MOLI bookstore; OCPs sell courseware directly to individual students or corporate clients. This model for instruction delivery has many interesting features, some also shared by communities such as Athena and GNA, but others that look quite new. Because MOLI has no physical infrastructure and few labour expenses, the cost of courses is low.

By carefully managing its third-party vendors, MOLI can effectively provide just-in-time training services; vendors move rapidly to create courses for new Microsoft products, to reach the market ahead of their many competitors. Also, like Athena and GNA, Microsoft is concerned with assessment exams and certification of students. However, in contrast to other virtual universities, MOLI has no concept of admission or courseload; students simply purchase instruction as needed (or as required by their employers), course by course, if not concept by concept.

Higher-Education Model

Training is a very different sector from higher education. Most training skills are relatively narrow and well-defined, whereas skills taught in higher education are usually broader in scope and more difficult to quantify. Business skills also typically turn over more rapidly than those targeted by higher education. Microsoft needs new courses every year for the many software products it creates, buys, or modifies; university classes often stay relatively fixed, in part because the topics they address-intellectual and cultural artifacts, from philosophy to algebra-change slowly, if at all.

The sectors also differ in the wealth of the clients they serve, as well as in the nature of the skills they target. Businesses routinely spend much more per worker on training than public education spends per student. Training providers can use this high profit margin to invest in new training technology, while higher-education institutions often find the price tag for new information technology too high. However, these differences are diminishing; indeed, previously distinct boundaries between the higher-education and corporate-training markets may be beginning to blur.

For one thing, higher-education institutions are coming under pressure to change their course offerings more quickly and to make them responsive to the demands of business. The resulting curricula often focus more on applied knowledge than do the ones they are supplanting. Corporate training is also moving in this direction, although from a very different starting point. In the past, most training schemes were vocational; today, more and more cater to knowledge workers in their never-ending quest for life-long learning.

Creative thinking and higher-order problem solving, topics once the exclusive domain of higher education, are slowly crowding out learning of routine procedures in training courses. Even now it is hard to distinguish, say, a computer-aided drafting course at a proprietary school from one offered by a community college or a university. At the same time, although today it is still easier to create courseware for training classes on programming and using spreadsheets, information technologies are becoming increasingly useful in education classes that focus on more-complex (and less-well-defined) problem-solving skills, as many of the Internet and Web tools we reviewed already attest.

Further, as these technologies continue to drop in price, higher education should become an increasingly profitable market for them. In short, education and training are merging in two senses: just as the content of training is becoming more like the content of higher-education classes, the feasibility and profitability of technology-based courses for higher education are rising to the level of computer-based training.

Information Technology and Higher Education

Several strands of evidence argue that proprietary providers already think that information technology has helped reduce delivery costs to the point where even "down-market" (read: higher-education) services can be delivered profitably. A growing number of companies now straddle both sectors, in many cases offering essentially the same courseware products to each.

For-profit companies are tapping each of them aggressively. Academic Systems is marketing directly to higher-education institutions. Others, such as The Teaching Company, look primarily to the home market. Many of them also offer educational software to corporate clients, for remedial instruction. Whereas, in the past, corporate training has focused mainly on job-specific skills, businesses now also are under increasing pressure to provide remedial instruction for employees.

In different guises, all these growing areas are calling for roughly the kinds of learning that higher education typically has offered. But, except in traditional higher-education markets (young adults coming straight out of high school), universities and colleges are largely ceding these opportunities to proprietary providers.

Higher-education institutions as a whole have not formulated plans to deal with the increasing encroachment of external providers on their "turf." They need to. These providers enjoy several advantages over higher education that enable them to devise creative systems for delivering training and education on the Internet and Web. To begin with, many are technically savvy and heavily capitalised. This means that external education providers often have both the financial and intellectual assets they need to experiment with high-risk/high-gain educational designs.

Perhaps more important, when designing schools or other delivery systems for learning, external providers have the great luxury of starting with a clean slate: no need, for instance, to assume that classes will meet at a set time, to worry about faculty displaced by software, nor to fight with teachers' unions. Consequently, when external providers craft their designs, they can focus on what the technology makes possible and what services their clients demand, rather than worrying about how to shoe-horn new designs into existing educational structures. At the very least, then, these providers offer innovative models for using information technology that higher education should attend to.

One approach is to shore up defences against invaders into traditional higher-education markets, for example, by erecting protectionist barriers that discourage new providers from entering the battle. Some would argue that the tax supports that public institutions now enjoy do just that. Perhaps a more positive tactic is to improve productivity in the face of new competition.

Many of the enterprises we have reviewed-distance-learning campuses and virtual universities, for example-can be regarded as ways in which higher education already is trying to become more productive, sometimes by borrowing models of delivery from the training sector, and often by creating innovative models of its own. A different strategy is to take the offensive, rather than honing defences. Inspired in part by movements of external providers into higher education's turf, a few institutions are beginning to respond to the challenges posed by external providers by moving, however cautiously, into contract training. Of all higher-education institutions, the community colleges have shown by far the most initiative here.

A few years ago, about half of all community colleges did some contract training with business; today, about 90 percent do. Some community-college experts even see training as the solution to their financial problems and expect that contract training will become the biggest piece of the community-college system. Still, higher education faces several imposing difficulties in this migration, some of them technical. Corporations, for example, expect personalised, on-site training services; external providers increasingly deliver these tailored courses through wired or even satellite-based network technologies.

Community colleges will need comparable tools in order to offer quality courseware at a competitive per-person price that is equally responsive to clients' needs. Other challenges are organisational, reflecting the fact that community colleges (unlike external providers) do not have carte blanche for building their contract training services. Business clients, for example, frequently expect to be able to mix their instructors with college personnel; however, doing so often conflicts with union contracts that forbid colleges to hire external staff.

Also, some contracting arrangements threaten informal or formal community-college rules requiring that the college serve mainly local needs (tough to adhere to if contract training is shipped across the state via networks) or demanding that classes be open to all students.

Corporate Training

While community colleges struggle to compete with external providers in the contract-training market, other higher-education institutions are starting to evolve different strategies, some involving cooperative partnerships as much as competition. In this battle, the size of long-established universities, while often a liability in times that demand nimble change, actually can work to their advantage. For one thing, some training needs are so vast that they attract only the largest providers.

For example, in 1996, Michigan announced a large-scale educational programme that would use the Web to deliver a wide range of courses. Centered around the Virtual Michigan Auto College (Auto U), the idea is to help train the next generation of auto-industry workers, and thus to keep the industry firmly centered in Michigan. This is far too big a training job for any proprietary training school to manage by itself, so the plan is to build Auto U as a collection of state schools, led by the University of Michigan and all tied together through the Web.

Auto U looks innovative from several perspectives. First, many courses will be designed by teams drawn from Auto U and business partners, giving business a muchstronger voice in curriculum planning than it usually enjoys. Second, the Internet apparently will play multiple roles here, beyond connecting students with instruction and linking businesses into course design.

Using Web sites connected to Auto U, the state's employment commission will provide instant access to all Michigan online automotive information for students and prospective employees. Students will even be able to take virtual occupation tours, learning directly from workers about the types of jobs available in plants today and the skills needed to do them.

In short, Auto U appears to have the key trait of healthy electronic-learning communities, beginning with one or two core functions, then quickly adding new functions and new stakeholder groups. The third innovative feature of Auto U is the addition of one such group: As well as public higher-education institutions, the Auto U partnership will also include some for-profit trainers. As such, it may be one of the first examples of a cooperative arrangement that includes higher education, external training providers, and business.

Since Auto U is still barely off the drawing board, it is too early to tell how this cooperative partnership between higher education and external providers will work. Several relationships are possible. Perhaps reminiscent of Athena, principal partners (the University of Michigan) might retain considerable control, contracting out specific courses or services to specialised providers; more like MOLI, the higher-education partners could manage, set goals, and ensure courseware quality while delegating much courseware development to external partners; even less constrained relationships, as exemplified by GNA, might work.

However, one common feature in all these possibilities is the role that the Internet and Web will play in tying together the different partners in this evolving community. Networks permit courseware and design discussions (as well as instruction delivery) to be shared readily, both within institutions and across their boundaries, enabling a collection of very different (and physically remote) institutions jointly to construct new educational curricula. Absent rich network connections, such heterogeneous models of education and training delivery simply were not feasible in the past.

Internet in Higher Education

At both high-school and college levels, some of the best intelligent-tutoring systems have fulfilled their goal of increasing the quality of student learning. Many distance-learning programmes in higher education, for example, have demonstrated that the cost of delivering courses can be reduced substantially while keeping student outcomes approximately constant. A few "augmented" distance-learning programmes have also improved student learning.

Algebra, geometry, and computer-programming tutoring systems developed at Carnegie-Mellon University, to take one of the most well-known successes, can raise scores on exams up to one full letter grade. On a broader scale, meta-analyses-which aggregate results of many separate experimental studies-show a smaller, but still statistically significant, effect of computer-based education.

In many ways, the data for corporate training are both simpler and more compelling than those for education. Most companies want to train employees to become competent in relatively well-defined skills. Improvements in proficiency in these skills can be easily measured. By the same token, it is easy to gauge how much is saved by delivering this training through video rather than using in-person instructors, as are the additional gains in flexibility and further cost reduction achieved by moving from conventional video to Web-based TV delivery systems. For many corporations, the results are impressive enough to justify investing billions of dollars each year in technology-based training.

But these clear successes of information technology in education and training are limited in many ways. First, as the examples from corporate training suggest, most of the solid evidence concerns a few very well-defined skills. Standard tests can reliably measure how accurately a spreadsheet is used, how fast an algebra problem is solved, and even how well a software routine is written. However, although these are valuable talents, they only scratch the surface of the kinds of abilities we want higher education, if not corporate training, to foster.

Complex skills-some specific to particular subjects, and others more generic, such as collaborative problem solving-are difficult to measure; therefore, it is difficult to show that information technologies improve how they are learned. But then, for these skills, it is currently impossible to demonstrate that any method of instruction delivery, whether it exploits the Internet or not, leads to improved learning. If this limitation disproportionately affects tools for learning and teaching that make heavy use of information technology, such as the Internet or Web, it is because they are often strongly associated with curriculum reforms that advocate teaching new, probably valuable but certainly ill-defined, kinds of knowledge.

A more straightforward reason for the scarcity of data demonstrating the value of Internet-based learning is that these applications are very new. While earlier generations of distance learning have acquired a certain pedigree with time, distance-learning courses that rely on high-bandwidth networks are now at most a few years old-barely enough time to turn a raw course prototype into a production-quality curriculum, let alone to collect a serious body of data showing how well students learn or how much schools might save. These facts lead to a broader point.

In general, the information-technology applications about which we know most are the ones that have been around the longest. Conversely, the newest Internet and Web applications have little evidence to prove, or disprove, their value for higher education. Unfortunately, these applications are the ones that, at least in theory and by logical argument, hold the most promise for confronting key challenges for higher education. So, anyone who insists on an airtight case before adopting a WWW technology will certainly be inclined to disregard, at least for now, some of the most cutting-edge ideas and applications.

Digital libraries that amalgamate holdings across institutions, individual publishing ventures, cyberspace lecture halls, electronic communities of practice, and virtual universities-none of these can claim yet to be sure bets for higher education. The question is how best to deal with this uncertainty. Plainly, an ultraconservative approach, one that accepts only proven technologies in higher education, is likely to be as irresponsible as a radical approach that embraces everything that looks appealing.

In the latter case, costly errors may be committed; in the former case, valuable opportunities may be missed. In deliberating this choice, it may be instructive to reflect on lessons that businesses have learned, often painfully, in integrating information technologies into the workplace over the past 15 years. To simplify only slightly, businesses generally have taken a very radical approach, early on adopting information technologies with relatively little forethought about which ones would best meet their needs or how they might change work practices.

As a result, it has taken many years-and many billions of dollars-to demonstrate that significant productivity gains were attributable to information technology. But, finally, these gains have materialised, partly through a careful evaluation of technology options, partly because the structure of the workplace has transformed to make the best use of these new tools, and partly because productivity itself has been redefined.

Higher education, now poised to take a similar plunge into information technology, can learn several lessons from these experiences. The first is that, eventually, the Internet and Web will probably live up to some of the promises offered by the examples we have reviewed. Second, it is likely that this success will materialise-slowly; that many applications that now appear to be most promising will not realise those promises; and, conversely, that some that will eventually succeed spectacularly are not even on the horizon today.

Third, many successful applications will require modest or substantial organisational change on the part of higher-education institutions. The resources required for such a radical strategy simply do not exist, even if traditional educational institutions had the stomach for such wild experimentation. Having let business bear the brunt of being the earliest adopters, higher education can, take a less radical and less costly approach and still reap the gains. But a substantial commitment is still required (not an ultraconservative strategy), and careful planning is needed to avoid as many pitfalls as can reasonably be foreseen.

On the surface, possibly the greatest barrier to moving higher education onto the Internet and Web in a big way is technical feasibility. Many higher-education institutions are now developing and implementing plans for distance learning around technologies having much less functionality than the Web will shortly offer-for example, videotape sent through the mail, one-way TV (over cable channels) augmented with two-way audio (through telephones), or two-way video-conferencing using special-purpose hardware.

To some of them, a proposal to use the Internet and Web for fully interactive, high-bandwidth, and multimedia courseware must look very premature. Perhaps, some will say, this is the Cadillac (if not the Mercedes) we all might be able to enjoy ten years from now, but we need to get started today-even if it means beginning with an Escort (if not a Yugo). It is true that many higher-education institutions have little Web presence at this time. California's community colleges, for example, represent over 100 schools and serve more than 1.5 million students per year, but as of April 1997, some of the schools were not connected to the Internet at all.

Of those that are wired, nearly one-half provide just brief electronic brochures advertising the campus and its mission. This is certainly a long way from the ample

Internet capacity education institutions will need to support richly interactive course materials and electronic learning communities. However, in one sense, this example is looking at the glass as half empty. Higher-education institutions, in general, are very well represented on the Internet, which is hardly surprising: For its first 25 years, the Internet was inhabited mainly by universities, nonprofits, and government agencies.

True, colleges and smaller universities still lag behind, but the larger schools remain among the most extensive and most sophisticated users of Internet and Web resources-even today, as commercial sites rapidly take over cyberspace. Web sites such as GNA and Athena already show that higher education can manage mid-sized, if not yet large-scale, Internet enterprises. Put most positively, the Internet is probably the only form of information technology with which higher education has more than kept pace with the business world, both in its raw capacity and its skill in creating useful products.

In one sense, then, to realise the many uses of the Web we have reviewed, higher education needs to preserve its position on the Internet more than it needs to gain new ground. However, commercialisation of the Internet and Web is sometimes viewed as jeopardising that position and as a threat to the small academic community that used to be cyberspace. Much of this concern is well-founded; today, most of the early, free-wheeling, and unregulated "electronic frontier" is long gone. One of the specific complaints against commercial expansion of the Internet, however, is that it will steal capacity, soon filling the pipes with cybercasts of Instant Baseball, for instance, and potentially crowding out quality educational material.

Maybe so, in the short run, but over the long term, commercialisation actually may benefit higher education in several ways. To begin with, capacity shortfalls triggered by huge increases in demand for Internet services are being met quickly, as providers rapidly lay down new fiber-optic cable and devise clever ways of using old physical infrastructure to meet new needs. All of this upgrading is being driven by the commercial sector, of course, but education can benefit too. Not only will this capacity expansion mean that educational material need not be crowded out; it actually suggests that education should have even more room in which to work than in the past, and better tools to make use of that capability.

One of the reasons skeptics view the Internet as an inadequate infrastructure for distance learning is that, even in its pre-commercial glory days, it did not supply the bandwidth needed to deliver rich instructional material, such as two-way video, in real-time. Today, for example, viewing short video clips using a 28.8K modem and a Web browser is a painfully slow experience-enough to make educators take refuge, again, in instructional TV. Commercialisation of the Web will change this.

A collection of new software and hardware products-from cable modems that provide hundreds of times the capacity of old phone lines, to digital wireless connections, to fractal compression algorithms that shrink movies so that they fit comfortably on old phone lines-will permit the Internet to carry interactive multimedia courseware, including video, from education servers to most homes and businesses. At the same time that commercial interests have expanded the capacity of the Internet, new tools, along with economies of scale, are causing prices to drop dramatically.

For example, video conferencing (in business as well as in educational settings) used to require special-purpose and costly hardware. Now it can be done equally well on the Internet, using ordinary PCs equipped with cameras (some machines come with cameras already built in) and running software tools such as CU-SeeMe. Although costs and features vary somewhat from site to site, Internet video conferencing probably costs, on average, about one-tenth the cost of special-purpose systems.

And this savings does not factor in the greater flexibility of Internet video conferencing: special-purpose video conferencing systems deliver instruction in only one way; networked PCs can be configured for video conferencing or for many of the other instructional models. In short, then, far from threatening higher education's position, commercialisation of the Web is providing the tools and capacity needed to create and deliver interactive, multimedia courseware at very low prices.

But knowing this is still a long way from saying how specific institutions should go about building their Web products, how they can be guaranteed the broadest and least-expensive Internet access, or how much it might cost to wire universities and colleges. Several recent studies have offered cost estimates for wiring primary and secondary schools on the information superhighway, describing the characteristics and prices of various connectivity models.

Coordinated technology plans and purchases. The simplest such strategy that higher-education institutions-actually, all educational institutions-should have is to change their model for technology acquisition. Today schools at all levels buy (piecemeal) hardware, infrastructure, software, and support services for computers and networking, usually through funding mechanisms that provide only small, yearly technology allocations and that rely heavily on intermittent donations from large foundations or corporations.

Sometimes these windfalls enable institutions to build impressive technology-intensive centers through substantial one-time investments. But to put together broad technology infrastructures, higher education would do much better to plan technology purchases more systematically, as corporations do, and especially to coordinate acquisitions across a whole campus, institution, or even a system of schools. Currently, telecommunication providers generally regard education as a collection of small, sporadic buyers of computing goods and services, rather than as large consumers whose purchases are driven by a well-designed technology plan.

As always, big, organised buyers will get much more for their dollar than small, inconsistent ones. This is a pity, because education is actually a huge industry, but one that is handicapped because of its fragmentation. By coordinating purchases around a coherent vision, higher-education institutions would obtain much better prices; perhaps more important, they could command the kinds of personalised services that only major industries such as aerospace and entertainment now enjoy.

Exploiting a window of opportunity provided by the Telecommunications Act of 1996. As important as it is for higher education to develop long-term technology plans and form large-scale purchasing alliances in order to negotiate effectively for Internet infrastructure, taking less-direct policy actions may be even more crucial. State and federal debates are now setting the stage for regulations that will influence the quantity, quality, distribution, and cost of telecommunication infrastructure and services over the coming decades.

New laws forged during these deliberations will certainly change the character of the Internet in many ways, potentially affecting educational applications just as profoundly as they do commercial applications. The centerpiece of this legislation is the Telecommunications Act of 1996. With the act's passage, many think the best window of opportunity for influencing policy so that it will benefit education is now gone. In fact, the act ignores several critical issues, delegates some decisions, and defers yet others to later dates.

A brief sampling of some of these still-open opportunities shows that Internet capabilities available to higher education, and their costs, could look very different, depending on the outcome of political fights still to come in Washington and state legislatures. In the best of all worlds, consumers would pay modest amounts to access courseware across the Web, regardless of distance, providers would have multiple paths along which to distribute their courseware, and both would be relatively free to use copyrighted material for learning purposes.

In the worst of all worlds, consumers would pay substantial sums to access courseware at a distance, providers would enjoy few options for distributing materials, and the content produced and consumed would be severely limited by extremely tight intellectual-property laws.

Table 1. The Telecommunications Act of 1996.

Issue	Implications for Education
Universal Service. The act provides only broad guidelines for universal service. The real fights will take place at the state level, between the FCC and Public Utilities Commissions.	Local battles will decide what universal service means now, and how it evolves over time. Eventually, it could include Internet and broadband access for all. Now, it just covers phone service.
Consumer Protection. Federal and state regulatory agencies still must set rules governing	These local battles will have direct effects on consumers' choices and rates. They may also affect Internet

competition in local phone (and often cable) markets. Long-distance companies are already fighting for a "modem tax."	costs, which are currently low and independent of distance. Long-distance phone companies are challenging this situation.
Intellectual Property. Decisions concerning intellectual-property rights were not addressed in the act. Congress is currently holding separate hearings on them.	At stake is whether current principles of fair use and public domain will apply to electronic communications. The current administration's White Paper would make even browsing copyrighted documents an infringement.
Spectrum Auctions. Spectrum decisions were initially part of the act, but were stricken at the last minute. At issue is whether networks will be granted spectrum for free, or whether it will be auctioned by the FCC (garnering tens of billions of dollars).	If the spectrum is auctioned, proceeds could be reinvested, for example, to wire schools and fund educational services. Alternatively, if the spectrum is not auctioned, TV networks could be required to dedicate fixed amounts of bandwidth to education and training.

Whether the world turns out closer to the best of all, or more like the worst of all, will depend, in part, on how effectively advocates argue higher education's case over the next year or two. Based on history, prospects look bleak indeed. While publishers, cable, and telephone companies have powerful lobbies in Washington, education's cause in the telecommunications-reform debates is being championed by only a few educational organisations and a handful in Congress.

When it comes to political advocacy, higher education is about as fragmented as it is in technology acquisition, and with similar results-or lack of results. However, if higher education could patch together its uncoordinated constituencies, it could achieve the size, and eventually the clout, of a powerful lobbying organisation such as the American Association of Retired Persons.

A group with even a fraction of that weight might help steer many ongoing telecommunications debates in favour of education. But to do so would require that different institutions unite behind a broad common vision of what they want to do in education and what technology tools are required to get the job done-to become, if necessary, a single-issue group that sends a consistent message about the telecommunications infrastructure it will need in the next century.

Internet-Based Education for Individual Learners

Even if higher-education institutions can secure the infrastructure needed to supply generous amounts of richly interactive courseware across the Internet, only one-half of the problem is solved. The rest will be accomplished when consumers-students of all ages-are able to interact comfortably and cheaply with these products. Many already can, of course. But, if education on the Internet is to be as readily available as education in the classroom, students of all ages will need almost universal access to online courseware. Today, this is not the case.

Assuming that cable TV, upgraded phone lines, or new wireless paths can bring the Internet to the door (admittedly a somewhat open question), students still need machines on which to display, process, and even create digital courseware. Right now, the only machine that does this is a personal (or bigger) computer, which, adequately equipped for Net surfing, costs little more than $1,000-about one-half what a comparable machine cost just three years ago.

Roughly one-third of U.S. households have at least one PC; however, while this number is steadily growing, the fraction is not changing very rapidly, in part because PCs remain several times more expensive than other information appliances, such as TVs. This means that the next decade, at least, will see a gap of 50 percent or more between the goal of universal access and the percentage of homes that are likely to have PCs.

Technology changes, ushered in by commercialisation of the Internet, certainly will shrink the gap somewhat. PC prices will continue to drop, which, combined with increases in computer demand, will draw some consumers on board. But, the advent of dedicated Internet appliances (at perhaps $500 per unit), or possibly Web televisions, is likely to more immediately increase Internet access. How much and how quickly it shrinks the universal-access gap is anyone's guess.

One generous conjecture might be that, within a decade, 75 percent of households will have some kind of Internet machine-about midway between the percentages of households with cable TV (65 percent) and with VCRs (85 percent). Given a serious commitment to universal access, policy instruments, rather than technological devices, probably will be needed to cut further into the remaining 25 percent gap. The policies that are appropriate will depend on who makes up this remainder.

Many ideas have been considered: Universities could supply machines for students (some already do); older computers might be recycled to low-income students; libraries and other community services could provide Internet access; manufacturers might consider pay terminals (analogous to pay telephones); and governments could use vouchers as well as other forms of cross-subsidy.

Suffice it to say that students most in need of help will have relatively low incomes and low education levels. In short, many of those who would profit most by Internet appliances will be least able to afford them.

Quality Courseware and Educate Faculty

If universities and students soon enjoy lavish Internet capacity, they still will need quality Web learning products that make good use of this capacity. To judge by current offerings, obtaining such products will take a long time. As any Net surfer knows, most Web sites offer little of value, and what useful educational products do exist are difficult to find, because they are usually "hidden" in isolated pages rather than combined into well-organised structures akin to textbook chapters or libraries.

Moreover, the first generation of tools for creating Web documents was far from user-friendly: Faculty who built homepages needed to be skilled word processors, understand the rudiments of HTML, have access to tools that translate files among several different text and video formats, and even programme in Java, in order to develop highly interactive educational products. In spite of these challenges, there are several reasons for optimism. First, Web-based courseware is already beginning to flourish, and sites such as the World Lecture Hall, GNA, and MOLI are adding several layers of organisation to these individual products.

In doing so, they are both facilitating access by students and making it easier for faculty to find and build new online courses. A related bonus is that courseware is becoming easier to construct, in part because much Web publishing is based on a nontraditional model for creating content: Instead of being created from scratch, new courses are often built from previous ones, using simple digital cut and paste-just one example of how the Web encourages rapid development by facilitating layering of products, one on another.

Layering means that individual faculty will be able to build much courseware using just simple editing tools;

not all will need to master the programming skills usually required to create courseware from scratch. Driven by a rapidly evolving commercial market, software vendors are now coming up with a new generation of tools that will automate much of the construction of Web courseware, so that it is becoming easier to create courseware from scratch when necessary. In the past, constructing even the simplest Web homepage required at least a bit of HTML coding.

Now faculty can use off-the-shelf tools to create many multimedia products with almost no direct programming. Some tools convert existing documents into Web-ready format; others build new homepages through dialogues with users; still others provide high-level graphical interfaces, delegating the synthesis of low-level HTML code to underlying software. Predictably, a few Web publishing wizards have put together sites that organise many of these diverse authoring resources, providing a valuable starting point for those interested in learning about them.

Finally, and perhaps most important, online information sources and support communities abound. They will help even the least-Web-savvy faculty member develop the necessary Web and Internet skills. These sources take several forms, ranging from simple FAQs, to detailed hypertext documents on the art of HTML programming, to newsgroups and listservs that engage in active discussions on how to provide Web services. All these are free. For a fee, any of hundreds of start-up companies that now offer Web product-development support will gladly design and implement Internet sites of any size, or will assist institutions or individual faculty in doing so.

Even if all these tools and supports help faculty become comfortable creating and teaching Web-based distance-learning courses, higher-education institutions will probably need to consider several kinds of changes and policies to smooth what might be a substantial transformation for many teachers. An obvious first step might be to offer courses that give faculty hands-on training with Web publishing technologies and, more broadly, that demonstrate examples of good Web courseware and principles for creating useful educational products on the Internet.

It is natural to expect that schools of education would continue to play a pivotal role here. Certainly they will need to revamp many programmes to help faculty acquire new teaching skills that are better suited to technology-intensive classrooms-classrooms that will be less dominated by lecture and more driven by collaborative projects or online mentoring. But to delegate all training on Web publishing, as well as on new teaching practices, to schools of education might risk duplicating services unnecessarily since, online communities are already poised to do much of the job and offer yet another example of new electronic communities that crisscross the boundaries of traditional higher-education institutions.

Higher education must find strategies for coordinating with such communities, if only because much of the literature and training they offer is good-and free. Although courses and electronic communities might help faculty acquire skills in Web-based courseware development, one big question remains: Skills can be acquired at roughly current levels of funding, provided faculty can reallocate the time they devote to their various teaching activities. Information technology is slowly beginning to displace some of the traditional teaching roles of faculty; students will spend more time working with smart software or watching digital lectures and less time listening to live discourses.

This shift might tempt some schools to cut staff and thus reduce costs, but an alternative would be for faculty to be retained and to use their newly freed-up time to play other roles. One role that may expand is intensive coaching, to help students learn when even rich interactive software is not enough. Or, faculty could spend more time creating courseware. Thus, one way to acquire better-quality online courseware, and to educate faculty to create and use it effectively, is simply to recommend that faculty be given more time and resources to engage in these activities.

If the transition from lecture-intensive curricula to Web-based courseware is managed reasonably, this added course-development time may come at little or no increased cost to higher-education institutions. In effect, the outlay should come out of savings in direct teaching costs. Nourishing grassroots publication. Higher-education institutions can also encourage the development of higher-quality Web courseware through tactics that help foster and manage the grassroots, or individual, publishing that is taking shape in online communities such as the World Lecture Hall.

Universities and colleges could follow GNA's lead and provide a common infrastructure for online courses. The fact that many contributions in these databases already come from higher-education institutions suggests that, even today, universities have much courseware to be organised. Perhaps they would do even better to copy proprietary institutions, e.g., MOLI, which supply such value-added services as establishing areas and goals for new courseware, offering technical assistance to courseware developers, and furnishing quality-control standards.

Setting standards for courseware format will probably be as important in the long run as setting content standards. If faculty develop materials in diverse formats that do not interoperate, the advantages of creating new courseware using simple cut-and-paste tools diminish greatly. Lecture overheads rendered in PowerPoint, for example, do not mix easily with Adobe Photoshop representations. On the other hand, if universities encourage faculty to build online courses that adhere to emerging Web-document standards, they will be inviting the sharing of course products.

One of the great strengths of the early Internet, veterans will say, is that intellectual products-software and ideas alike-were shared freely. The past was never really quite so grand, but it is true that the tradition of "freeware," "shareware," and "open systems" has been strong on the Internet, and it will probably continue to be essential, in some form, if individual publishing in higher education is to prosper. This culture of sharing faces several threats, and higher education should keep them in mind, if not actively work to keep them in check.

However, individual faculty publishers also should have protection for their intellectual products. Many professors already make substantial sums selling courseware. As with big publishers, they too may be reluctant to share their materials without being compensated. As always, the challenge is to strike a balance that rewards innovation enough to keep new ideas flowing while also maximising the social benefits of those new ideas.

Individual faculty, their institutions, and higher education as a sector have yet to work out clear policies that define a feasible balance point. These decisions are tough enough when restricted to a single college or university but take on added complexity when courseware is shared across institutions or even states, not just within them.

Virtual universities, such as the World Lecture Hall and MOLI, will catalogue courseware from any publisher that meets their standards, regardless of location. In so doing, they recognise that one of the most powerful features of the Internet is that it encourages the free flow of ideas and course materials to any place in the country-an idea that most states and public universities have yet to come to terms with.

Such free flow is perhaps the biggest issue higher-education institutions will have to face in the near future. State and academy barriers are much tougher to defend against "invading" software than national barriers are to defend against, say, illegal aliens. Laws will need to be rewritten to reflect the fact that courseware that might be in college online catalogues will probably be derived from, or even wholesale copies made from, products found in other university databases. Nor should such sharing be viewed as simply bowing to the inexorable forces of network technologies that make editing and transmitting digital materials virtually effortless.

If managed properly-for example, through careful quality controls and well-organised cataloguing services-the net effect of promoting such sharing can be a dramatic gain in the quality of Web-based courseware. One cost of this freedom, of course, will be that the boundaries between different institutions may begin to blur, at least when it comes to course offerings, if not social functions and research reputations. Such blurring suggests that, in the future, some universities might be more brokers of education, reminiscent of MOLI and GNA, than full-service providers.

NEW DELIVERY MODELS FOR EDUCATION

Dominant Model of Delivery

The dominant model of delivery in higher education is still one-stop shopping: A single provider offers all educational services at a single location. But this model may be challenged for dominance. New information technologies add substantially to the set of models that providers can consider.

Broadly, these models unbundle educational services and repackage them in different ways. Some highly specialised providers offer only a few courses rather than large sequenced collections, some broker courses rather than creating them, and others create and deliver courses, but in partnership with several providers rather than solo. While mass education, including primary and secondary schools, vocational and training institutions, and colleges and universities may be the most common formal method of learning, many of us remember taking piano or dance lessons from highly specialised providers.

Although marginal in this country, intensive apprenticeships have persisted as powerful learning methods for centuries-so much so that many hope that information technologies soon will make cognitive apprenticeships feasible on a large scale. And new information technologies are not the only reason different models of education delivery are beginning to flourish.

Growing markets for adult-learning services require changes in traditional delivery models; consumers of on-the-job training, for example, insist on courses that are highly tailored to specific needs, rapidly changeable, and delivered at the workplace, not in the classroom. New information technologies are supplying most of the raw materials from which delivery models that meet these demands can be fashioned. In the past, regardless of demand, it was prohibitively expensive to consider, say, creating courses for a widely scattered and relatively small group of consumers.

Now distance matters little in the economics of such services. And whereas, once, only the largest corporate-training clients could expect house calls from education providers, today size counts for much less, because on-site education can be done mainly through high-bandwidth network virtual visits. Time is also less of a factor: House calls from education providers never came on demand; now educational courseware can be accessed across the Web 24 hours a day.

Processes and Products

The idea that information technologies can (and should) radically transform processes and products seems routine in discussions of manufacturing and service industries, but the idea that the Internet might help reduce costs of courses or improve the quality of students' learning still draws doubts from thoughtful pundits such as Larry Cuban, Neil Postman, and Clifford Stoll. But no one questions that the same tools help produce lower-priced, higher-quality cars. The view that technologies could help speed the creation of courses or help build courses tailored to specific learners seems original and offbeat, yet just-in-time manufacturing is familiar to anyone with even a passing knowledge of business.

And while the idea that a monolithic education institution might be unbundled into a collection of services may sound altogether foreign, it is the industry conglomerate that sometimes looks out-of-touch with modern views that businesses often do much better by specialising, and perhaps partnering with others to develop products.

Education-Delivery Models

The different models of education delivery enabled by new information technologies such as the Internet and Web might be to try to systematically attempt to characterise the vast range, or space, of alternatives. However, doing so would probably be as cumbersome as trying to describe all the ways that businesses could restructure using new technologies.

Knowledge chunks: Why are courses so long? Courses in higher education usually extend across many weeks. Quarters and semesters vary in size across institutions, but not radically. And within institutions, there is little variation at all. Courses offered to corporations by external providers, on the other hand, often last no longer than a few hours and are driven by the needs of the client and requirements of the material, rather than by the conventions of the providers.

One-size-fits-all courses certainly make bookkeeping easier for degree-granting institutions and probably are impossible to circumvent if classes must meet at scheduled times and places. But if students learn mainly at a distance, can choose to start a course when they wish, and can access courseware anyplace, anytime, perhaps courses of variable length, tailored to the needs of the subject are feasible.

Course flexibility: Why offer only a few courses per subject? Why not add to course listings in an ongoing fashion? Most universities and colleges change their course offerings slowly compared with MOLI and GNA. On the surface, increasing speed of course creation and the diversity of courseware could only help consumers, assuming value-added counseling services were available to help them select the products that best match their current level of expertise, educational goals, and learning styles.

Tools that permit faculty to rapidly create new Web products certainly will help expand the range of courseware a university offers. However, MOLI and GNA enjoy even more flexibility, because they invite outside developers to develop online materials. Whether or not institutions can offer a large pool of courses, therefore, will probably depend on changes to other structural features, some of which are noted below.

Why limit class enrollment: Most university courses place caps on the number of students they will admit, and on the size of individual classes. In prestigious institutions, this often means that demand outstrips supply in ways that more market-driven service industries never see. Recent experiments at the City University of New York and long-term successes at the Open University indicate that distance-learning technologies can open up enrollment while keeping costs under control and quality reasonably high.

As demand for quality adult education continues to grow, various models of "partially open" enrollment might be worth considering. A school might, for example, allow anyone to take a distance-learning course on the Web for a nominal fee, subject to the constraint that he or she access only online resources. Students could also pay additional fees for more labour-intensive services, such as online tutoring and proctored exams.

12

Optical Media

Optical media are used for storing digital sounds, images and data. There are three main families:

— The commercially issued, mass produced, CD family including the digital audio CD- both 12cm and the "single" 8cm disc—CD-ROM, CD-I and CD-V and the analogue Video Disc.

— Optical disks and tapes that can be recorded on once.

— Re-recordable disks.

Jukeboxes are available for most types of disc allowing automated access to a number of discs.

Mass Produced Discs

The mass-produced discs of the CD family have the digital information in the form of microscopic pits pressed into a polycarbonate base which is coated with a light reflective layer. This reflective layer is usually of aluminium, but gold and silver are also used. A transparent lacquer is then placed over the reflective surface to protect it. This surface also carries any label information.

As the data on members of the are impressed, they cannot be altered or rewritten. Because of the high costs to setup the production of a pressed disc, the discs are only used when large numbers of copies are required, for example, encyclopaedia or sound recordings. The higher the number of discs issued, the lower is the unit price. The storage capacity of a 12cm CD is about 650 MB or one hour of audio. The average access time is about 300 ms with a double speed player, 250 ms with quadruple speed and 130 ms with sextuple speed.

The first disc in the family to be developed was the 30cm analogue LV (Laser Vision) Disc for video. This usually consisted of two discs stuck back-to-back to form a double sided disc with one hour of video per side. A sub-format was developed which could store up to 54000 still video images per side. The LV disc was the most successful of several attempts to generate market acceptance but is expected to be superseded by the DVD (Digital Versatile Disc or Digital Video Disc) that is being launched in 1997. The DVD is the same diameter as the CD (12cm) but, by using a laser with a shorter wave length, the storage capacity of one layer is increased by a factor of seven to 4×7 GB.

Additionally, a dual layer structure will be possible, read by two different laser wave lengths, thus doubling the capacity to 9 GB. In principle, by glueing two such double layer disks together like the LV video disks, a total capacity of 18 GB can be achieved. The disk is intended for the storage of data-reduced video-films or, like CD-ROMs, texts and multimedia data with, however, considerably higher storage capacities.

Write-Once Recordable Media

There are several types of write-once recordable disks. The format that is becoming the most widely used is the recordable CD (CD-R or CD-WO) which has been available since 1993. Having the same format and storage capacity as the audio CD and the CD-ROM, the CD-R can be played on the appropriate standard CD drives. The polycarbonate body of the disk has a dye layer placed on it which is then coated with a metallic reflective layer. The dye layer carries the data in place of the pits of pressed discs.

When recording, high-intensity laser pulses change the dye from opaque to transparent. The low-intensity read laser reads the changes in reflected light as a digital bit stream. Once written, the data cannot be altered. CD writing drives are already available on different speed levels. The CD-R is a well established and standardised format. Different standardised software protocols are available for recording Audio CDS and CD-ROMs. The Photo-CD is a CD-R with a proprietary software protocol to record photographs as electronic still images.

A recordable version of the DVD in not yet available, but may be expected in the near future. CD-Rs are but the latest and most prominent examples of so-called WORM (Write Once, Read Many) disks which have been in use as computer storage media for quite some time. The biggest problem with WORMs is the great variety of systems and formats. A number of producers offer WORMs with a continuous helical recording format similar to a sound LP disk; others offer disks with ring-shaped tracks as on computer floppy and hard disks.

Some can use both formats. The proprietary software of WORMs poses a problem, too. Not even the physical dimensions are standardised. One writing method used by a number of manufacturers including LMS, Toshiba and Sony burns pits in the metallic surface of the disc with a laser beam. Another system supported by ATG and Optimen creates bubbles by the heat of the laser beam. In both cases the reflectance of the metallic layer is changed and the data can be read by a low power laser beam.

Optical Tape

Optical tape is made by ICI and packaged in a cassette for use as a WORM format data storage tape. The tape drives are made by EMASS in the USA and supplied in Europe by GRAU Storage Systems. Kodak are about to launch a competing system. The tape contains a dye layer which changes its state when a high power laser beam is applied and can be read by a lower power laser - the same basic method as for CD-Rs. Because the tape is a sequential carrier, the access time can be quite long. In compensation, the storage capacity of one tape is considerably greater than a disc (up to 100GB).

Re-writable Optical Media

In contrast to the preceding optical media, data on re-writable optical disks ("Erasable"), Magneto-Optical (M/O) and Phase-change, can be altered or deleted many times. There are re-writable optical disks in the 5×25 inch format and, more recently, in the 3×5 inch format. The most common still are the magneto-optical discs, where a laser beam in the write mode heats the inner layer of the optical disk and thus changes the polarity of a magnetic coating. The resulting microscopic magnetic marks of different polarity can be read as a bit stream by a low-energy laser beam in the read mode.

A more recent recording technology is the Phase-change where the carrier layer is coated with a thin semi-metal film, which can be both in an amorphous and in a crystalline state. A laser beam in the write mode can change single spots to either an amorphous or a crystalline state so that, again, a digital bit stream is created. The

Phase-change may replace M/O in the future. Re-writable optical disks have a short access-time (600 milliseconds). The storage capacity has steadily increased up to the current 2×6 GB.

Stability of Optical Carriers

The main factors that affect the stability of carriers and the retrieval of information can be summarised as:

— Humidity and temperature.

— Mechanical deformation.

— Dust and dirt of all kinds.

For some carriers there are additional factors:

— Light

— Stray magnetic fields.

Humidity is, as with other data carriers, a most dangerous factor. In the case of optical media it has a hydrolytic action on components such as the protection layer of CDs and a corrosive influence on all metal components including metallic reflective layers. As a secondary effect, high humidity levels (above 65% RH) encourages the growth of moulds and fungi which can obstruct the reading of optical information. Temperature, as with all other data carriers, determines the speed of (deteriorating) chemical reactions. More importantly, it is responsible for dimensional changes which may be of concern, especially in the case of multi-layer media.

Mechanical integrity is of utmost, and underrated, importance. Even microscopic scratches can hinder the reading laser beam, as do fingerprints and other foreign matter. Mechanical bending of discs cause microscopic cracks which again divert the laser. While the WORM and MO-disks developed as computer storage media are housed in cartridges which only open when inserted into the respective players, the representatives of the CD-family must be handled with utmost care, keeping mechanical integrity in mind.

Dust and dirt prevents the proper reading of the recorded information. Cigarette smoke will accumulate on the disk surfaces and may hide information. The CD-family is again more exposed to this danger than those disks that are protected by cartridges.

Light may affect the dye layers used in recordable and erasable disks. Stray magnetic fields must be kept away from magneto-optical disks.

Recommended Climatic Storage Parameters					
	Temp	±/24h	±/Year	RH	±/24h
Optical Media	about 20°C	±1°C	±3°C	40%	±5%

Fluctuations of chosen parameters should be kept to a minimum. Operation areas (studios) should, therefore, have the same climatic conditions as storage areas. As with magnetic carriers, tighter parameters would be favourable for long term preservation. Such suggestions have, however, to be offset against the availability of hard- and software, which seems to be of greater concern than the stability of the carriers themselves.

Standards

AES28-xxxx: Draft AES Standard for Audio Preservation and Restoration - Method for Estimating Life Expectancy of Compact Discs (CD-ROM), Based on Effects of Temperature and Relative Humidity.

AESxy-xxxx: Draft AES Standard for Audio Preservation and Restoration—Method for Estimating Life Expectancy of Magneto-optical Disks, Based on Effects of Temperature and Relative Humidity.

13

Virtual Reality in the Library Environment

The library as a building has been transformed to the library as an environment of electronic services established on a computer server or a network of cooperating servers. The client is not obliged to go to a certain place for searching and retrieving his information, since the information is coded in a binary form being available to any person linked locally or through the Internet to the specific server.

Copies of a book are real entities stored somewhere in the selves of a library and each of them can be taken and read by a user. In the virtual environment, the notion of the "copy" has been eliminated, since the information is omnipresent to any person equipped with communication link, communication protocols, and decoding software compatible with the one used by the stored information. Types of resources have also been expanded. Print is no longer the only way of representing information.

Texts, still images, video, audio (sounds, music and speech), and any combination of types are just some of the information carriers in the multimedia era. Resources are digital from the beginning or they are the digitised version of corresponding analog forms. An ongoing transition to digital repositories through immense "retrodigitisation" programmes is taking place.

Electronic resources are also available on the Internet (commonly indicated as Networked Information Resources or NIRs). Although access to most NIRs is currently uncontrolled and free, controlled access (e.g., through user registration and passwords), and fee-based access (based on networked payment mechanisms) are options, which allow the addition of commercial and copyrighted materials to the range of networked information resources.

Electronic documents differ radically from printed ones. Printed documents are typically distinct entities of a static, unchanging nature. Initially, electronic documents were just imitations of printed documents in electronic form. Recently, they have become more and more compound and dynamic. Compound means that the document can consist of various distributed "information objects," discrete components, each of which can be at a different physical location. It can also include metadata (e.g. author, revision history, etc.) and links to external multimedia modules (images, video, audio, graphics, etc.).

An electronic document can be nothing more than a set of pointers to a number of components. Dynamic means that any component of the document can change, giving the document a temporary nature. It is obvious that the up-to-date nature of a NIR is its strength but also its weakness. It is exactly what someone needs in a rapidly changing world and at the same time is something that cannot be used as a reliable and constant citation, since the reliability of a resource can be assured only by its maintainer.

Another critical factor in the effective use of the resources is the foundation of a common ground of standards, which is absolutely necessary for the improvement of their interoperability. The concept of interoperability includes wide usefulness (re-usefulness), portability (across networks, systems, and organisations) and longevity (portability across time). The key to the interoperability of content is consistency, and consistency is achieved through the use of standards.

The working environment of electronic resource collections is still called a library. Such a library is called digital or virtual, namely, "a library that provides access to a collection of distributed information in electronic format through pointers provided locally ... or a collection of digital objects housed in the same place, virtual or physical". A digital library is also described as "a zone of convergence where librarians, computer scientists, electrical engineers, cognitive scientists, cultural anthropologists, organisational theorists and sundry others are forging a lingua franca for better understanding the nature of distributed information systems and knowledge access".

The digital libraries sector is a rapidly developing area, combining many areas of research and technology. From a database or information retrieval perspective, digital libraries may be seen as a form of federated databases. From a hypertext perspective, digital libraries could seem like a particular application of hypertext technology. From a wide-area information service perspective, they could appear to be one use of the World Wide Web. From a library science perspective, they might be incorporated in the trend toward library automation.

Obviously, a digital library is not confined to any of those fields but it must be considered a union of subfields with great added value, because one can participate more actively in searching and retrieving information in a relatively controlled environment. A digital library remains a library incorporating the existing tradition of physical libraries, but at the same time offering new capabilities, impossible in the previous conventional environment. Following this view, we can make use of the physical library elements as a starting point for discussing the elements and domains of digital libraries, considering three broad classes of library elements: data, metadata, and processes.

Access to Networked Resources

At the present, libraries tend to use the existing cataloguing rules for the bibliographic control and access to networked resources. This is a natural decision, since it requires relatively little change in familiar practices and procedures and a low investment in systems. In the future this approach will not be satisfactory, since it will provide little support for the complicated task of networked cataloguing and offer the user less functionality and ease of use.

Thus, there is an urgent need for a new generation of library systems, designed to cope with the requirements of integrated networked services. It is a question whether automated digital libraries can rival conventional libraries today. Let us see the contrast between web search engines and conventional abstracting and indexing services or library catalogues. The selection of material indexed by a web search engine is automatic based on arbitrary considerations, there is no authority control, and the content can contain many dead links. On the other hand, cataloguing is expensive, while web indexing is cheap.

The leading web search engines index several hundred million web pages every month, more than the total number of MARC records that have ever been created. Since it depends on the priorities set by the user. The new kind of resources demand a new set of skills, and even an entirely new relationship with publishers. During the negotiation process between the librarian and the publisher, the librarian must agree to certain restrictions on photocopying or distribution of electronic materials. The library is responsible for maintaining the awareness in all employees about copyright issues.

The number of electronic resources is increasing rapidly. Libraries are paying more attention to their ability to get access to these resources than to archiving and protecting print materials for users in the future. Unlike a print book or journal, electronic resources cannot be considered permanent additions to a collection. It is not the product itself that is purchased but access to the product. The publisher and not the librarian dictates how much access will be provided, which issues will be available, and how much access will cost.

Data, Metadata, and Processes

Data are library materials, metadata is information about them, and processes are functions performed over library elements. We can find digital library data corresponding to physical objects. Texts, still images, videos, and recorded audio can be digitised and stored in the memory of the server. When translating a book into a series of digital images, all of its information is retained except perhaps some exceedingly specific details. Conversion of a printed book into ASCII text to be used in full text retrieval is followed by the need for considerable decision-making and labour regarding its final form: various fonts and letter sizes, graphics and images will be lost, since only the basic text is preserved.

A classification scheme such as Library of Congress Classification is an example of metadata. A classification scheme does not have any physical reality itself, but its application is sometimes constrained by the physicality of the objects it classifies. Sometimes it is used as a guide to the physical location of data in a library, since placing similarly-classified objects in physical proximity can aid patrons in locating data.

We can see here the superiority of the virtual library, whose abstract space can be used for multiple classifications of a book, a fact impossible in the frame of a physical library. An example of a physical library process a librarian helping a patron find something for which he or she has incomplete information. This process is necessary in an integrated virtual environment, since digital library patrons cannot rely on being near someone who can help them.

While the digital library starts at the physical level, it continues with elements and services absent from the physical library environment. Hypertext and active computational objects are examples of new library data. Multiple classification schemes are examples of new library metadata. Lastly, sophisticated human-machine interfaces used for more efficient and userfriendly communication and adapted also to users with special needs are an example of new automated library processes.

Digital Libraries Initiative

The Digital Libraries Initiative (DLI) is a major US government initiative funded by the National Science Foundation (NSF), the Defense Advanced Research Projects Agency (DARPA), and the National Aeronautics and Space Administration (NASA). Projects of the DLI pursued deep semantic interoperability, uniting heterogeneous items in a single uniform federated source. In the net of the 21st century there will be a billion repositories distributed over the world, each belonging to a certain community.

Semantic indexes operated through scalable semantics and concept switching will be effective in bridging the gaps between the specialised terminologies of the various communities.

The arbitrarily hyper-linked Internet will be gradually transformed into a semantic Interspace. For the extension of web searching beyond full-text retrieval, document structure in the short run, and document semantics in the long run, are required. The expanded resource type in the digital library environment has had an unavoidable impact on the query and retrieval processes. The Informedia DLI project at Carnegie Mellon University led to a terabyte digital video library. Automatically derived descriptors were used for indexing, segmenting, and accessing the library contents.

Speech recognition, image compression, face and colour detection, and video optical character recognition (VOCR) combined in a very sophisticated manner resulted in an effective multimedia retrieval mechanism. In general, the query techniques used in the digital library environment will be the result of an optimal integration of traditional library facilities and current web-based approaches.

The virtual nature of resources could relate them to the ancient concept of Platonic eidos/idea. Capurro gives a very interesting interpretation of the concept of information through its etymological connection to the concept of form. Information in this sense is the process of forming a piece of matter or, metaphorically, human knowledge.

Shannon and Weaver in their mathematical theory of communication establish a neutral, independent of the human comprehension, meaning of information content. Carl Friedrich von Weizsaker relates this neutral substance, which is neither matter nor energy to the Platonic eidos and the Aristotelian form. Therefore, information content is meant as an autonomous substance, which drives every kind of process, a pattern archetypon for the changing or informing something. We can consider the virtual resource as the information content beyond and before any information process.

The virtual resource coded in a machine language and stored in a machine memory can be transformed to a human sensed resource through the process of information. Something existing but not sensed by the human factor can take many forms, either on the screen or printed, conveying meaning to the human. This can be considered as analogous to the platonic eidos, something not accessible by the human senses, which can take a multitude of material forms, comprehensible by some species of material life, including human.

14
Issues of Library Environment

The library as a building has been transformed to the library as an environment of electronic services established on a computer server or a network of cooperating servers. The client is not obliged to go to a certain place for searching and retrieving his information, since the information is coded in a binary form being available to any person linked locally or through the Internet to the specific server.

Copies of a book are real entities stored somewhere in the selves of a library and each of them can be taken and read by a user. In the virtual environment, the notion of the "copy" has been eliminated, since the information is omnipresent to any person equipped with communication link, communication protocols, and decoding software compatible with the one used by the stored information. Types of resources have also been expanded. Print is no longer the only way of representing information.

Texts, still images, video, audio (sounds, music and speech), and any combination of types are just some of the information carriers in the multimedia era. Resources are digital from the beginning or they are the digitised version of corresponding analog forms. An ongoing transition to digital repositories through immense "retrodigitisation" programmes is taking place.

Electronic resources are also available on the Internet (commonly indicated as Networked Information Resources or NIRs). Although access to most NIRs is currently uncontrolled and free, controlled access (e.g., through user registration and passwords), and fee-based access (based on networked payment mechanisms) are options, which allow the addition of commercial and copyrighted materials to the range of networked information resources.

Electronic documents differ radically from printed ones. Printed documents are typically distinct entities of a static, unchanging nature. Initially, electronic documents were just imitations of printed documents in electronic form. Recently, they have become more and more compound and dynamic. Compound means that the document can consist of various distributed "information objects," discrete components, each of which can be at a different physical location. It can also include metadata (e.g. author, revision history, etc.) and links to external multimedia modules (images, video, audio, graphics, etc.).

An electronic document can be nothing more than a set of pointers to a number of components. Dynamic means that any component of the document can change, giving the document a temporary nature. It is obvious that the up-to-date nature of a NIR is its strength but also its weakness. It is exactly what someone needs in a rapidly changing world and at the same time is something that cannot be used as a reliable and constant citation, since the reliability of a resource can be assured only by its maintainer.

Another critical factor in the effective use of the resources is the foundation of a common ground of standards, which is absolutely necessary for the improvement of their interoperability. The concept of interoperability includes wide usefulness (re-usefulness), portability (across networks, systems, and organisations) and longevity (portability across time). The key to the interoperability of content is consistency, and consistency is achieved through the use of standards.

The working environment of electronic resource collections is still called a library. Such a library is called digital or virtual, namely, "a library that provides access to a collection of distributed information in electronic format through pointers provided locally ... or a collection of digital objects housed in the same place, virtual or physical". A digital library is also described as "a zone of convergence where librarians, computer scientists, electrical engineers, cognitive scientists, cultural anthropologists, organisational theorists and sundry others are forging a lingua franca for better understanding the nature of distributed information systems and knowledge access".

The digital libraries sector is a rapidly developing area, combining many areas of research and technology. From a database or information retrieval perspective, digital libraries may be seen as a form of federated databases. From a hypertext perspective, digital libraries could seem like a particular application of hypertext technology. From a wide-area information service perspective, they could appear to be one use of the World Wide Web. From a library science perspective, they might be incorporated in the trend toward library automation.

Obviously, a digital library is not confined to any of those fields but it must be considered a union of subfields with great added value, because one can participate more actively in searching and retrieving information in a relatively controlled environment. A digital library remains a library incorporating the existing tradition of physical libraries, but at the same time offering new capabilities, impossible in the previous conventional environment. Following this view, we can make use of the physical library elements as a starting point for discussing the elements and domains of digital libraries, considering three broad classes of library elements: data, metadata, and processes.

Access to Networked Resources

At the present, libraries tend to use the existing cataloguing rules for the bibliographic control and access to networked resources. This is a natural decision, since it requires relatively little change in familiar practices and procedures and a low investment in systems. In the future this approach will not be satisfactory, since it will provide little support for the complicated task of networked cataloguing and offer the user less functionality and ease of use.

Thus, there is an urgent need for a new generation of library systems, designed to cope with the requirements of integrated networked services. It is a question whether automated digital libraries can rival conventional libraries today. Let us see the contrast between web search engines and conventional abstracting and indexing services or library catalogues. The selection of material indexed by a web search engine is automatic based on arbitrary considerations, there is no authority control, and the content can contain many dead links. On the other hand, cataloguing is expensive, while web indexing is cheap.

The leading web search engines index several hundred million web pages every month, more than the total number of MARC records that have ever been created. Since it depends on the priorities set by the user. The new kind of resources demand a new set of skills, and even an entirely new relationship with publishers. During the negotiation process between the librarian and the publisher, the librarian must agree to certain restrictions on photocopying or distribution of electronic materials. The library is responsible for maintaining the awareness in all employees about copyright issues.

The number of electronic resources is increasing rapidly. Libraries are paying more attention to their ability to get access to these resources than to archiving and protecting print materials for users in the future. Unlike a print book or journal, electronic resources cannot be considered permanent additions to a collection. It is not the product itself that is purchased but access to the product. The publisher and not the librarian dictates how much access will be provided, which issues will be available, and how much access will cost.

Data, Metadata, and Processes

Data are library materials, metadata is information about them, and processes are functions performed over library elements. We can find digital library data corresponding to physical objects. Texts, still images, videos, and recorded audio can be digitised and stored in the memory of the server. When translating a book into a series of digital images, all of its information is retained except perhaps some exceedingly specific details. Conversion of a printed book into ASCII text to be used in full text retrieval is followed by the need for considerable decision-making and labour regarding its final form: various fonts and letter sizes, graphics and images will be lost, since only the basic text is preserved.

A classification scheme such as Library of Congress Classification is an example of metadata. A classification scheme does not have any physical reality itself, but its application is sometimes constrained by the physicality of the objects it classifies. Sometimes it is used as a guide to the physical location of data in a library, since placing similarly-classified objects in physical proximity can aid patrons in locating data.

We can see here the superiority of the virtual library, whose abstract space can be used for multiple classifications of a book, a fact impossible in the frame of a physical library. An example of a physical library process a librarian helping a patron find something for which he or she has incomplete information. This process is necessary in an integrated virtual environment, since digital library patrons cannot rely on being near someone who can help them.

While the digital library starts at the physical level, it continues with elements and services absent from the physical library environment. Hypertext and active computational objects are examples of new library data. Multiple classification schemes are examples of new library metadata. Lastly, sophisticated human-machine interfaces used for more efficient and userfriendly communication and adapted also to users with special needs are an example of new automated library processes.

Digital Libraries Initiative

The Digital Libraries Initiative (DLI) is a major US government initiative funded by the National Science Foundation (NSF), the Defense Advanced Research Projects Agency (DARPA), and the National Aeronautics and Space Administration (NASA). Projects of the DLI pursued deep semantic interoperability, uniting heterogeneous items in a single uniform federated source. In the net of the 21st century there will be a billion repositories distributed over the world, each belonging to a certain community.

Semantic indexes operated through scalable semantics and concept switching will be effective in bridging the gaps between the specialised terminologies of the various communities.

The arbitrarily hyper-linked Internet will be gradually transformed into a semantic Interspace. For the extension of web searching beyond full-text retrieval, document structure in the short run, and document semantics in the long run, are required. The expanded resource type in the digital library environment has had an unavoidable impact on the query and retrieval processes. The Informedia DLI project at Carnegie Mellon University led to a terabyte digital video library. Automatically derived descriptors were used for indexing, segmenting, and accessing the library contents.

Speech recognition, image compression, face and colour detection, and video optical character recognition (VOCR) combined in a very sophisticated manner resulted in an effective multimedia retrieval mechanism. In general, the query techniques used in the digital library environment will be the result of an optimal integration of traditional library facilities and current web-based approaches.

The virtual nature of resources could relate them to the ancient concept of Platonic eidos/idea. Capurro gives a very interesting interpretation of the concept of information through its etymological connection to the concept of form. Information in this sense is the process of forming a piece of matter or, metaphorically, human knowledge.

Shannon and Weaver in their mathematical theory of communication establish a neutral, independent of the human comprehension, meaning of information content. Carl Friedrich von Weizsaker relates this neutral substance, which is neither matter nor energy to the Platonic eidos and the Aristotelian form. Therefore, information content is meant as an autonomous substance, which drives every kind of process, a pattern archetypon for the changing or informing something. We can consider the virtual resource as the information content beyond and before any information process.

The virtual resource coded in a machine language and stored in a machine memory can be transformed to a human sensed resource through the process of information. Something existing but not sensed by the human factor can take many forms, either on the screen or printed, conveying meaning to the human. This can be considered as analogous to the platonic eidos, something not accessible by the human senses, which can take a multitude of material forms, comprehensible by some species of material life, including human.

15

Theory of the Digital Library

The digital library is seen by some as a threat to the book, and a threat to the book is an attack on culture itself. Self-interest enters the fray because in the instability provoked by the digital library there will be winners and losers, whether in business, or the professions. Depending on your point of view the digital library can be the end of libraries as we know them, or the salvation of libraries as we know them. The growth of digital libraries has been phenomenal. Since then, the World Wide Web and its associated products and standards brought about a sea change whereby digital library projects now are simply too numerous to mention.

The Internet has famously changed the world of information without much formality of that kind. It could be argued that market forces have led us to the present state of the art and can be relied on to lead us further. One compelling software invention can overturn a mass of theory. On the other hand, it is argued, principles of information management hold firm whatever the technology, and practitioners just need to adapt themselves to the new techniques in order to proceed.

One of the early authors on the electronic library, and we note here that the terms electronic library and digital library are synonymous, was Kenneth Dowlin who wrote a book entitled "The Electronic Library" in 1984. He defined the characteristics of the electronic library as follows:

— Management of resources with a computer

— The ability to link the information provider with the information seeker via electronic channels

— The ability for staff to intervene in the electronic transaction when requested by the information seeker

— The ability to store, organise, and transmit information to the information seeker via electronic channels

There is nothing to disagree with there, so given the date of the work, this characterisation stands up quite well. However from a perspective thirteen years on we say much more. In 1991 when we started ELINOR at De Montfort we used the following working definition:

— A teaching, learning and study environment in which learning resources are held primarily in electronic form

That definition was intended to convey that a book library, however highly automated, is not a digital library. A library becomes digital when the majority of its resources are held in electronic form.

— A managed environment of multimedia materials in digital form, designed for the benefit of its user population, structured to facilitate access to its contents and equipped with aids to navigation of the global network

The virtual library, on the other hand, does need to be defined. It is the extension of the digital library to a state where there is no single physical access locale and there may be no single point of electronic storage. One can imagine a virtual library where the users and the holdings are totally distributed and the answer to every search is assembled "on the fly". We can imagine it, but we cannot see how at this stage such an entity would be managed, and we have said already that a requirement for the digital library is that it should manageable. However let us hazard the following definition for the virtual library:

— An electronic library in which the users and the holdings are totally distributed, yet still managed as a coherent whole

Returning to the question of whether definitions and theory are needed, the quick answer is that if there is no digital library theory, there would be no profession of digital librarianship. More important is the recognition that whilst some principles of information management endure, information technology has changed the world. All revolutions cause turbulence and anarchy, after which there is a new order. We are at that stage in library and information services. Some extremely basic issues about the digital library must be addressed, namely:

— We have to manage it

— We have to fund it

— We have to legislate

The last few years have seen massive development. From a situation only six or seven years ago where digital libraries were the tentative proposition of a few enthusiasts and often regarded with scepticism and hostility, they are now receiving endorsement and support at national and international level. For instance the eLib programme in higher education has now funded over sixty projects involving the majority of UK universities.

This programme has had a massive impact on strategic thinking in the university sector, not only on how libraries will develop, but more fundamentally on how teaching, learning and scholarship will be conducted in the digital age. What everyone seems to agree is that learning will become more student centred and resource based. Academic libraries have tended to lead digital library development, but the above lessons apply equally to public libraries.

However we must recognise that public libraries have a special role to play in the emerging information society. In the last analysis academic libraries exist to serve their host organisation and their direct customers: staff and students. Public libraries underpin the literacy of the people, access to information supporting citizenship and democracy, and of course leisure and culture. As public libraries become more engaged with the digital library than hitherto, even more fundamental questions will be asked and lessons learned which affect the fabric of society.

In Britain, the Library and Information Commission, has launched a public library networking plan, entitled "New Library: the people's network" which will propose to government a national infrastructure of communications, training and content to modernise public libraries for the next century. Already the Secretary of State has welcomed the proposals stating that they could be a defining moment for public libraries.

Characteristics of the Digital Library

In order to understand the magnitude of change which our theory of the digital library must encompass let us try to describe the characteristics of the digital library and to do so independently of the library environment: academic, national, public or commercial.

— Access to the digital library is not bounded in space or time. It can be accessed from anywhere at any time.

— Content in electronic form will steadily increase and content in printed form will decrease

— Content is in textual, image, and sound form

— Usage of electronic information as a proportion of total usage will steadily increase, and usage of printed material as a proportion of total usage will decrease

— Expenditure on electronic material will steadily increase and, relatively, expenditure on printed material will decrease

— Expenditure on information will shift from ownership to subscription and licensing

— Expenditure on equipment and infrastructure will increase

— Usage of buildings will shift from stockholding to places for study, animation and citizenship

— Jobs, training and recruitment will be re-profiled

Issues

Funding

Funding for new technology has always been a problem for libraries. As library automation developed over the last thirty years budgets have changed substantially to the extent that information technology infrastructure is now a major item. Although adjustment for automation was often difficult in tight fiscal circumstances, the problem was eased because it could be handled incrementally over time. With the advent of the digital library we do not have so much leeway.

Electronic information gets added to the portfolio

without corresponding reduction. Generally speaking libraries do not envisage huge improvements in budgets to allow for digital information. Digital information may well expand at the expense of printed information, which would be a painful process and exacerbate the polarisation of books versus electronic materials. However we should look more widely than the library budget.

In universities, for instance, there is much talk of developing student centred, resource based learning, both on pedagogic and on financial grounds. We are not yet seeing the restructuring of teaching and learning, together with the associated restructuring of expenditure away from teacher centred activity towards resource based activity. This will surely have to come. As organisations move towards being learning organisations, or knowledge based organisations this type of restructuring will need to occur in many types of enterprise.

Returning to the library, a new library economy will need to be developed. It is not enough to say that electronic information is expensive, without making valid comparisons with the alternatives and measuring the relative cost benefits. These could be intangible, but nevertheless hugely important.

— Licensing versus ownership, over time

— Payment by usage versus subscription

— Space requirements in the electronic environment

— Equipment and communications

— People, their changing skills and remuneration

— Co-operation with other providers, including the private sector

— Income generation, publishing and charging

All of these factors will need to be compared with the traditional library economy, including all the associated overheads of print-based libraries, which are often ignored.

Free or fee

The debate as to whether libraries should offer fee based services, or be free at point of use has intensified with the development of online and business information services. The totally electronic library will require this issue to be faced more than ever before. As a point of principle, this is most sensitive in public libraries, but it is an issue for all. As the electronic information market grows ever larger, and budgets remain constrained, the pressure for income generation will become more intense.

Authority

Authority is an important issue for the quality of library services. In the past we relied on the process and the reputation of publishers to provide document authority. Authority was further supported by the librarian, who by professional and subject knowledge guaranteed the integrity of the collection. In the electronic world this authority us threatened in two ways:

— Proliferation of unvalidated documents

— Possibility of alteration of documents

The former is of course not new, but it is the scale of the problem which will require attention in our new theory. The latter we can reasonably expect to be solved by emerging watermarking and "cryptolope" techniques such as those developed by IBM, but in an increasingly commercially driven world our theory will need to alert librarians to the risks of supplying incorrect material or that which infringes copyright or paternity rights.

Censorship

Librarians have long been supporters of freedom of information and against censorship in general. It is one of the basic principles of librarianship. There is, however a growing recognition that the unprecedented availability of pornographic, violent and otherwise illegal or undesirable content will require new policy approaches in the electronic library. Whereas in the past, librarians would protect children through their acquisitions policy, the electronic library will require active, preventative measures.

Social inclusion

Like many new developments, the electronic library has potential for both positive and negative outcomes. Nowhere is this more critical than in the area of social inclusion. For instance, information technology is raising great expectations for improving access for the disabled, through specialised applications and through home access. People in rural areas or in minority community groups now have opportunities for access to information in general or to specialised local services. At the same time the gap between the rich and the poor, at least in Britain, is widening and there is a clear danger that the increasing commercialisation of the library and information market will exclude sections of the community. On the wider scale, the ever increasing dominance of the English language threatens global cultural diversity.

Democracy and citizenship

In various countries, there is a strong tradition of support for freedom of information. From central government there has been a tradition of secrecy, often taken to absurd lengths. This reminds us that in Britain we are subjects, not citizens. However we have great hopes that our new government with its high ideals and huge majority will promote citizenship through information. This is one of the main thrusts of our proposals for the "People's Network". On the global level, the electronic library, which transcends borders, is potentially a great safeguard against secrecy, propaganda and disinformation.

Libraries as publishers

Many of these big issues lead to the realisation that libraries have the opportunity, more than that, the responsibility to publish. The technology is not a problem. Public libraries are the natural collectors and publishers of government, community, cultural and leisure information at the local level. University libraries may yet decide to publish their faculty's academic work rather than utilise the existing supply chain.

Two Internet sites in particular were helpful, namely Rutgers and Berkeley. Some of the topics are of course carried forward from traditional library management. Others are entirely new or are not new, but have not hitherto been of such central importance to librarians. This leads to a set of assumptions which perform two functions.

— Of course the digital library must be electronically stored and accessed

— It must be quality assured as to authority, stability, and legality of content

— It must manage access and ownership

— It must be designed for its users

— It must be financially manageable, which means that costs must be predictable, controllable, sustainable and acceptable

— It must provide sophisticated facilities for navigation

locally and globally, providing effective searching and avoiding duplication

— It must provide assurance to copyright holders of good practice and protect from infringement by staff and users

— It must provide facilities to track, control and pay for usage, whether or not usage is paid for at point of use

— It must provide facility for human intervention for help and management purposes.

If we can elaborate the body of theoretical and practitioner knowledge around these principles, and developing a theory of the electronic library. This will provide both a cultural and economic framework within which digital library professionals can form principles of good practice for operational purposes and for ongoing training of our people.

16

Changing Trends of Libraries

The library is a database and information retrieval system. Digital libraries are a set of electronic resources and associated technical capabilities for creating, searching, and using information. In this sense they are an extension and enhancement of information storage and retrieval systems that manipulate digital data in any medium (text, images, sounds; static or dynamic images) and exist in distributed networks. The content of digital libraries includes data, metadata that describe various aspects of the data, and metadata that consists of links or relationships to other data or metadata, whether internal or external to the digital library.

Digital libraries are constructed—collected and organised—by [and for] a community of users, and their functional capabilities support the information needs and uses of that community. They are a component of communities in which individuals and groups interact with each other, using data, information, and knowledge resources and systems. In this sense they are an extension, enhancement, and integration of a variety of information institutions as physical places where resources are selected, collected, organised, preserved, and accessed in support of a user community. These information include, among others, libraries, museums, archives, and schools, but digital libraries also extend and serve other community settings, including classrooms, offices, laboratories, homes, and public spaces.

Access to Information

Access to information is an essential prerequisite of the digital library to operate and be successful. Access can be seen to have three aspects:

1. *Connectivity*: to a computer network. Using the digital library depends entirely on the ability of users to connect to a network to access it.
2. *Content and services*: 'connectivity is useless without them'. If the digital library contains insufficient content, and the services it offers do not meet the needs of users, then there will be little interest in accessing the digital library.
3. *Usability*: of the digital library and of the network. Digital libraries and services which are too difficult to use will not thrive.

Other aspects of access to digital information are also important. One is the problem of preservation of digital information. Digital libraries have enormous potential to 'enhance access to knowledge, to support learning and education, to promote progress in the science and useful arts'. This is exactly what public libraries also do. Digital libraries can allow libraries to do this better. Some specific aspects of libraries and relate them to the digital library are:

— Changes in publishing

— Usability

— Organisation of content & union catalogues

— Copyright and ownership

— Libraries: physical place or virtual space?

— Which formats?

— Types of libraries: public, academic, special.

Changes in Publishing

Electronic publishing is already with us. It has the same requirements as the digital library—to be successful, both electronic publishing and the digital library need widespread computing and widespread networks. Electronic publishing has already proved to be cheaper than print, distribution is faster and wider than traditional paper-based publishing, and all the signs are that these trends will continue. It is possible that electronic publishing will almost completely replace print publishing. This has implications for libraries. It suggests that 'libraries and publishers as we know them, will no longer be needed, as people will acquire their own content directly from computer networks'. The continuity scenario, on the other hand, is that 'libraries will continue to be necessary to select, collect, organise, conserve, preserve, and provide access to content, in many media'.

Usability

One impediment in the way of digital libraries becoming more widespread is that they are not yet easy to use. Digital libraries need to be 'easy to learn and to use' and need to be designed for usability. How do we do this? One way is to design them for a specific community, whose information needs are understood. Examples are legal researchers, employees of a specific company, or students at a specific university. The users' information requirements, level of expertise, and information-seeking behaviour need to be understood so that the digital library can be tailored to their needs and so can be more usable and therefore more effective. There are four main ways to make digital libraries easier to use:

Link metadata to data: In the past, digital libraries contained only metadata, and mainly textual metadata. Online databases such as those available on Dialogue are examples. The techniques and software developed for searching these databases were good at retrieval of metadata, but they were not—and are still not—very good at retrieving full text. When we try to use these search techniques for other digital information, such as images, the retrieval is even less effective. But we want our digital libraries to be useable for searching a wide range of digital information, not just text but images, videos, and sound, and so we have to develop more effective techniques for searching and retrieval.

We also need these techniques and the software to be easy to learn, and also easy to relearn for the user who only needs to use it occasionally. We also need to accommodate expert users as well as beginners. We need 'simple interfaces that are easily learned and relearned by novice and intermittent users while providing sophisticated capabilities for expert searchers'. These are not available at present.

Link digital libraries together: Linking together multiple digital libraries will provide greater access to more information sources, offering a better result to users.

Provide navigation capabilities rather than searching capabilities: Classical information retrieval methods are less effective with full text than with metadata, for which they were developed. Two areas where research is needed to make this aspect more effective are user interface design, and intelligent assistance.

Allow the digital library to be interactive: Research into information seeking behaviour has typically studied individuals, but it is now clear that most information-related activities involve more than one person, and that these people interact. However, the digital library as it is structured at present does not cope with this interactivity. Examples include negotiation with customers (for example, reference interviews), and team work (for example, group researching of a problem and group writing of a report about that research). We need to improve the digital library in this area.

ORGANISING INFORMATION

Organising information is an important function of libraries. To do this, information must be described, represented, and organised so that people can discover its existence, locate it, and obtain it. Libraries have a long tradition of organising information. For example, in the United States libraries began sharing cataloguing information over 100 years ago. This lead to the development of international standards in libraries for cataloguing, to international sharing of cataloguing data by computer (the MARC record is an important standard for this), and currently to the international development of standards for metadata to organise a wide range of information, not just library material.

Currently 'libraries have more experience with creating, maintaining, and distributing metadata' than any other group. Libraries have constructed large databases of metadata (cataloguing records) such as bibliographic utilities like OCLC, and libraries provide access to material in libraries nation-wide through the use of these large metadata databases. A union catalogue is a single catalogue which combines the records of several catalogues. OCLC is one example. OCLC is the Online

Computer Library Center and is based in Dublin, Ohio, in the United States. OCLC's online database of MARC records is used by libraries in all parts of the world to download cataloguing data, and to locate publications.

Libraries have very great expertise in managing such union catalogues in electronic form. Online union catalogues such as OCLC 'represent a significant step toward creating a global digital library of metadata indicating what information resources exist and where they are located'. They allow users to discover whether the information being sought exists, and where it is located. Libraries and librarians have very significant experience in developing and maintaining such online union catalogues (or databases of metadata). Currently this expertise is lacking by those who are constructing digital libraries, who often come from a non-library background.

Libraries can contribute effectively in this area to the development of digital libraries. In fact, it can even be said that this library expertise is essential to allow digital libraries to reach their full potential. In Borgman's words, 'the necessity for mechanisms to identify, locate, and obtain information is increasing with the proliferation of digital content in many forms, in many languages, and in many places'. However, we need to be aware of some problems. One problem is that library practice and library standards have been developed for print-based material. They work best with paper publications and with older media such as films and photographs.

They cannot always be applied effectively to digital material, especially to material created digitally ('born digital'). Another problem is that metadata is increasingly being created 'upstream', that is by the authors, creators, publishers and producers of digital material. Library practice develops the metadata after publication. Librarians are playing a role (and can continue to play this role) in the development of metadata standards for digital material.

COPYRIGHT AND OWNERSHIP

In the print-based publishing world and in traditional libraries, copyright and ownership were more-or-less under control. We all understood the laws which governed copyright and we knew who had the legal right to copy, even if in some countries these laws were not obeyed. These laws were developed for printed material such as books, and worked well for them. When easy ways of copying, such as photocopiers, were widely available in libraries, copyright laws started to become unenforceable. With the introduction of information in digital format, there has been a change from libraries owning material by purchase or legal deposit, to libraries licensing the rights to material for a specified period.

PHYSICAL PLACE OR VIRTUAL SPACE

One definition of a library is 'an agency that selects, collects, organises, preserves, conserves, and provides access to information on behalf of a user community'. Libraries have evolved over many hundreds of years to serve the information needs of their communities. Most libraries are closely linked to a defined community, and nearly all of them are closely defined by a physical building or physical location. In the 1990s there has been a resurgence of interest in libraries as physical places. This may seem odd, given that there was also a very strong interest in the opposite, digital or virtual libraries, in the 1990s.

Many new libraries have been built, 'designed to support the latest technologies while preserving existing materials in multiple formats'. Examples include many large public libraries in the United States: Los Angeles, San Francisco, Cleveland, and new national library buildings: in France, Germany, and the British Library. What is significant is that these libraries combine traditional functions with new ones: in Borgman's words, 'the new model for library services is not a print library or a digital library; it is a hybrid ('mixed' or 'composite') with complementary print and digital collections'.

Even at a more local library level, in public libraries in many countries the user can visit to borrow a book or videotape of CD, and during the same visit also use the Internet. The opposite is also possible, of course. However, what is different in the new hybrid library world, compared with the world of traditional libraries, is that the user does not need to visit the library in order to use some of the library's services. The catalogue can be accessed online, some full-text material can be read online, books can be located and reserved, video clips can be viewed, photograph collections can be browsed, and so on. Many library users are now using the library without visiting the library's building.

Libraries have traditionally dealt with paper-based information: printed books, manuscripts, journals, pamphlets, maps, newspapers, and so on. Now much of the information previously available only in paper format is now available in digital versions. The digital version may sometimes exist in addition to the paper format, and sometimes instead of the paper format. Although some people have prophesied that paper formats will disappear, there is very little sign of this happening. Lancaster's vision of the 'paperless office' is an example; another is the lack of interest in attempts to promote e-books (electronic books) in the American market in the last three years.

Many libraries, perhaps most libraries, will in the future maintain physical collections of paper-based material as well as other material in other physical formats (videotapes, CDs, and so on). What will decide the balance between information held in physical formats, and information in digital form, which the hybrid library will provide access to? The answer to this question is: the community formed by the users of the hybrid library. The formats must be those which are most usable to that community.

Types of Libraries

Different types of libraries have different communities of users, and therefore have different roles to play. The use of public libraries is growing throughout the world. Public libraries serve a very diverse community, potentially everyone in the community from the very young to the very old, from different ethnic groups, speaking and reading many languages, and with varying levels of education and knowledge about how libraries operate. The community can visit the public library and use its services, including access to computers and to the Internet. Some people in the community may not be able to afford as access to computers and the Internet, so the public library plays an important role in providing them with access.

For public libraries, it is likely that the function of library as physical place will remain very important. The role of academic libraries is defined by the mission of the school, university or research institute. The community which uses an academic library is well defined and has specific needs. These users are more likely to have access to networked computers. They will use the library's facilities from networked computers based in offices, dormitories, houses and hotel rooms, as well as from computers based in the library.

The academic library will also have collections of physical formats, and in the case of long-established large university libraries, these physical collections are large—for example, measured in the millions of volumes. Services offered by academic libraries are expanding as the possibilities increase, as more information resources become available in digital form, and as more users have access to networked computers. Examples of services offered are electronic publishing, electronic reserve collections of journal articles, digitised lectures available though the library's Web site, and online tutorials about how to use the library.

Information resources previously available only in print are often now available in digital forms, with improved access such as the ability to search them. Manuscript material can be digitised and made available. Special libraries are rapidly becoming digital as their parent organisations move online. As one example, the librarian in a company library is often the person who maintains the company's Intranet. Another example is where material is created online in a company, such as building plans or product designs, and they are delivered to the company's library online, and accessed online. There is no paper copy.

Digital Data Preservation

In the world of digital libraries, digital preservation looms as one of the greatest challenges of information management technology and policy. A number of solutions are being proposed, such as migration, emulation, and maintaining computer museums of all combinations of hardware and software. All the solutions proposed so far have serious drawbacks and all are likely to be expensive... Society is in greater danger of losing its records and artifacts in digital form than losing those in physical form.

All of us in this room will know about the way in which computers and digital data are now central to our lives. Many of us use information from the Web, we word-process letters, we take photographs using a digital camera. At our place of work, we communicate by email, we search and perhaps maintain electronic databases, we develop lists of contacts and store them electronically.

Christine Borgman suggested that 'physical libraries will be replaced by digital libraries'. Even if paper-based material and other non-digital formats take a long time to disappear from library collections, we already have large quantities of information in digital form in our libraries. We subscribe to databases and journals in electronic form. We digitise material and mount it on our library web site. We need to learn more about this digital information, especially how to make sure that we can keep it for long periods of time. We already know that paper can survive for many hundreds of years, and we know how to help it survive for long periods, for example by storing it in stable conditions at low temperature and low relative humidity. We do not know how to do this for digital information.

Digital data have considerable advantages. But these benefits come at a cost. So what's the cost? Why am I sounding an alarm? The problem is that it is much more difficult to keep information in digital form for the length of time that is either required by law, or for as long as users require access to it. For example, we know that high quality permanent paper (that is, paper which is manufactured to meet permanent paper standards such as ISO 9706 'Information and Documentation—Paper for Documents—Requirements for Permanence') will last for a minimum of 100 years, and up to 500 years.

The life of microfilm which has been processed and stored to archival standards is measured in centuries rather than decades. But even the most optimistic of estimates indicate that digital data, for example data stored on CD-ROM, will not last beyond 100 years. There are two main areas of concern, Media degradation and Loss of functionality of access devices.

Media degradation: What happens here is that the storage media (the diskette, magnetic tape, CD) becomes degraded and the data on it becomes unreadable. Factors which cause this include:

— Storage under high temperature conditions

— High relative humidity during storage

— Cleanliness of the storage environment

— Inappropriate handling

— Media coming into contact with magnetic materials

— Disaster (e.g. lightning strike)

— Wear caused by use

— Manufacturer defects

— Equipment faults.

Librarians do a lot more than provide fiction for people to read through public libraries. Some librarians consider that keeping information for the future—preservation—is the paramount duty of the library profession. The primary duty of the information worker is to ensure that he and his clients have access to information media which record what they want to know, and that the information is recorded in such a way which makes it both physically and intellectually retrievable. Librarians can't link users with the information they seek unless that information is available. Therefore, librarians have to ensure that the information stays available.

There are three main methods of digital preservation:

— Technology preservation

— Technology emulation

— Information migration.

— Keeping the artefact

The first strategy is technology preservation. This means that we maintain museums of working computers. It is generally considered not to be possible to do on a large scale, as a computer processing environment (the software and manuals in addition to the hardware) is almost impossible to preserve indefinitely as a working museum artefact. Experience in the U.K. has shown it to be prohibitively expensive, even when the systems it was supporting were very valuable. Technology emulation is a term used for preservation of the computer operating environment.

It is also considered to be only a short-term solution. What happens is that software is developed for a current model computer; this allows you to run software for an older, often completely different kind of computer on it. Much of the research in this field has been directed towards emulation of computer games. A list of emulations available for games includes Atari, Nintendo and Sega in various flavours. Very recently an American scientist, Jeff Rothenberg, in conjunction with Dutch information professionals, has been experimenting with emulation as a technique to be applied in libraries and archives.

Migration is the main strategy being developed and used to preserve the information. It breaks the connection between the data and the technology to read that data, so that technological obsolescence is no longer a concern. Migration is the periodic transfer of digital materials from one hardware/software configuration to another, or from one generation of computer technology to a subsequent generation. The purpose of migration is to preserve the integrity of digital objects and to retain the ability for clients to retrieve, display, and otherwise use them in the face of constantly changing technology.

In essence this means that when we upgrade our computer systems, we must have in place a well-planned strategy for upgrading all of the data we want—in other words, we migrate it to the new system. It is vital to note that it is not just data representing the information content which we need to migrate. It is essential that we also preserve a range of other information, such as contextual information about it (a programme, a business record, metadata) and technical information about how to access it (such as details about the programme used to create it) and about it should be displayed.

Other strategies have also been used, although they are suitable only for a limited range of digital information. We can transfer the information to longer-lasting media: printing out to paper, or computer output to microfilm are two examples of this. These are only suitable for flat files. What about complex multimedia digital information, such as Web sites? Printouts of these represent only a small percentage of the information they contain. The strategies which will work in the future are not about technical computing or data storage issues.

These will change rapidly—we know that and we have largely discarded it as a way towards reaching viable solutions to the preservation problem. They are about management issues—how to plan for archiving at the creation stage of digital records, how to ensure that someone takes responsibility for archiving the electronic journals when the publisher goes out of business, how to manage the process of migrating data from one system to another, how to manage a backup procedure for a large computer system, how to do the same for our own PC at home.

Most of us have, as yet, little practical experience of data migration or data salvage, but this is changing. Some organisations such as the National Archives of Canada and the (U.S.) National Archives and Records Administration have now had decades of experience, a 'standard practice' has not yet been defined. We are getting closer—but we aren't there yet.

PANDORA Project

Many large organisations are already actively involved in preserving digital data. In Australia, the National Library of Australia established the PANDORA Project in 1996. PANDORA stands for Preserving and Accessing Networked Documentary Resources of Australia, and can be located on the Web at http://pandora.nla.gov.au/pandora. Since its establishment in 1996 its achievements include:

— establishing the PANDORA Archive of selected Australian online publications such as electronic journals, organisational sites, government publications and ephemera

— developing policy and procedures for the preservation of, and provision of access to, Australian online publications

— developing a proposal for a national approach to the long term preservation of these publications.

In late 1998 the National Library of Australia sought industry feedback about its proposals, and last year issued a request for tenders for a computer system which would meet its requirements.

InterPARES Project

Several international research projects are developing better strategies for preserving digital data. One of these is the InterPARES Project. The InterPARES Project is based at the University of British Columbia in Vancouver, Canada. It focuses particularly on records, that is, transactions between governments, organisations and individuals. Many of these transactions (records) are now created electronically and never existed in any other form. As one example, consider buying a book from the online bookshop Amazon.com. One searches the database of books online, places the order and pays electronically, and receives notification by email that the book has been sent.

More and more government business is being carried out electronically, and this will increase. Many of these records have to be kept, some of them permanently, for administrative, legal and cultural reasons. The InterPARES Project is investigating how electronic records can be preserved in a way that ensures that their content is accurate and can be relied on as authentic. It is doing this by carrying out a series of case studies of electronic records systems, from which are being developed the requirements for systems which will ensure the authenticity of the electronic records which it preserves.

What can we, as individuals, do about these significant and threatening issues? At the least, we can be aware of them and discuss them more widely with others so that general consciousness about them is heightened and decisions we and others make are better informed. We can ensure that we have in place good data storage, backup and migration procedures for our own data, especially the data which we do want to last a long time. We can encourage our employers and the organisations to which we belong to think about and put in place good data storage, backup and migration procedures.

Librarians are taking this problem of preserving digital information very seriously. Jobs are now being advertised which are largely or solely concerned with digital archiving. For example, you could recently have applied to be the Coordinator of Digital Archiving and Preservation at Harvard University Library. In February 2000 the National Library of Australia advertised a position as Manager, Digital and Audio Preservation. The library profession is taking this matter very seriously.

Cost of Digital Libraries

The Web, of course, continues to grow, and the cost of computing equipment continues to decline. Traditionally, communities (universities or governments) paid for basic library services for their members, with some special services (e.g. photocopying) being fee-based. The Web is world-wide, however. Every university librarian is being asked "why should our university pay to maintain such-and-such a Web service, when most of the users are not our students, faculty, or alumni?" The situation is aggravated by the desire of some publishers to bypass libraries. Every business now admires the ability of the airlines to charge different prices for the same commodity, and thus get more money from those more able to pay.

Publishers would like, ideally, to identify each reader of their publications and extract the maximum payment from each one; why, instead, let them pool their resources, buy only one copy for a library, and hide their marketing demographics? Organisationally, we do not know who will provide information to scholars in the future. Technological transitions often mean a change in the organisation that provides them: Western Union does not run e-mail, the railroads do not fly airplanes, and Winsor & Newton does not make photographic film. Will "digital libraries" will be run by traditional library organisations or by publishers, or by somebody else? There is no shortage of people that want to be in this niche: publishers, bookstores, wholesalers, telecommunications companies, computer centers, and new startups.

Nor do we know whether there will continue to be as many libraries as there are now. In a world where every town's restaurants, drugstores, and clothing stores are merely instances of national chains, the independently run public and college libraries seem almost an anachronism. The organisational solution depends on the economic one. How will digital information delivery be funded? Among the possibilities are:

1. Communities pay the full cost.
2. Readers pay by the month or year (subscription fees).
3. Readers pay by the item received (by transaction).
4. Authors pay (page charges).
5. Advertising pays.
6. Other (bounties, cost avoidance, publicity values).

Community Support

Steve Harnad has argued at great length that digital publication is so cheap that community support for free information ought to be affordable. ARL statistics, very roughly, would suggest that the yearly cost of a research library per book is in the range of $3-8, and that per staff member a library might have 7,000-20,000 books. If we assume that a book is about 0.5 MB on average, that means that a typical cost is at least $5 per MB, and that each staff member keeps track of not more than 10 GB. By contrast the San Diego Supercomputer Center manages disk, even replicated for safety, at something like $3000 per terabyte or. one-third of a cent per megabyte.

The Internet Archive also has prices in the cents per megabyte range and with thousands of gigabytes per staff member. A fairer comparison to these data facilities might be an offsite deposit library, such as the Northern Regional Library facility of the University of California, which keeps track of some 2 million books with about 20 staff, or some 50 GB per person. Similarly, the Center for Research Libraries has about 4 million books and an annual budget around $4M, or about $1 per book and $2/MB. Even these numbers, although about a factor of 5 better than a library providing the usual academic services, are a factor of 100 larger than computer storage.

So digital storage sounds really cheap, as it should with the raw capital cost of disk space running at $179 for 120GB in the summer of 2002, or 0.15 cents per megabyte. That's a tenth of a cent a book-equivalent, whereas building a book storage building, even as a warehouse, runs about $2/book. But it's not that simple. The numbers above suggest that a repository library is 1/5 the cost of a normal university library. This means that most of the cost of a library is in services—cataloguing, reference, circulation and the like—and not in the cost of keeping the building heated and painted and answering the occasional request to fetch a book.

Nobody who works in a library will be surprised by that. Unfortunately, the implication is that you can't save all that much money by reducing the cost of storage via digitisation. If 80% of a library's cost is in services, not storage, even reducing the storage cost to zero leaves the library needing 80% of its budget. Well, maybe digital libraries won't provide any services. Google can be used instead of a catalogue, acquisitions can be done with robot web crawlers, and people looking for reference help can be told to get lost. For expert researchers, that might be of use in some situations.

It's not a strategy likely to be thought appropriate or adequate for a university which has a responsibility to teach students. We'll have to hope that it is not widely adopted in response to financial pressures. There are some savings possible in services. Libraries can share digital files more easily than paper copies, so some of the acquisitions tasks might be shared. And some of the digital material replaces paper material and comes with its own cataloguing and the like; for example JSTOR has been deliberately designed to substitute for back-issue files of traditional serials. JSTOR estimates that libraries could save \$140M/year by substituting its service for traditional paper storage.

So far relatively few libraries have discarded journal issues because JSTOR holds them, but many do move the journals to cheaper storage. Unfortunately the attempts to share also destroy locality. If the resources provided are not used solely by the community paying for them, why should the community pay? In the past, the number of visitors from one library to another has been relatively small, and whether or not they were charged fees, the impact on the library budget was small. Today the majority of the users of a university site may be outsiders, and they are likely to come from all over the world. For example, the British resource site BUBL (digital library resources for the UK) got only 15% of its identifiable accesses in July 2002 from UK sites.

So why should any university provide a good rather than minimal digital library service? This is the "tragedy of the commons" once again, on a global scale. The danger is that each university will try to cut its library budget, hoping the students will find what they need elsewhere. Fortunately, the library community is very strong in both its public service ethic and its inertia, which should keep things going until the economists can figure a way out.

Subscription Sales

Another possibility is that digital library services can be provided on a cost-recovery basis. Certainly many publishers are trying this. So far, success is limited. The poster child for Internet subscriptions is the online Wall Street Journal.

The Wall Street Journal has more paper subscribers (over 2 million), and Consumer Reports as well (over 4 million). The paper prices are higher ($175/yr for the Wall Street Journal, and $26/yr for Consumer Reports), so the discrepancy in revenue is even larger than the discrepancy in subscription counts, but this is still a substantial on-line subscriber base. If everyone paid full price (there are discounts available in both paper and online modes), the Wall St. Journal would get about 15% as much from online as from paper, and Consumer Reports almost 20%. A key choice publishers must make is whether to price for individuals or libraries.

Clearly, both the Wall Street Journal Interactive Edition ($79/year, less if you subscribe on paper as well), and Consumer Reports ($24/year) are priced to permit individuals to subscribe. But other publications such as JSTOR or Elsevier's "Science Direct" are priced only for libraries. Reed Elsevier reports that in 2001 ScienceDirect sales were up 50%, and their revenue in 2002 from online sales will top $1.5B, so the library subscription model is working here, thanks to elaborate definitions of who is allowed to access material.

An example that may be more relevant from the standpoint of scholarly publishing is the ACM Digital Library, which offers access to all the ACM journals and proceedings online for approximately $100/yr. This is again an individual price, affordable by many individual members of the ACM (a U. S. professional society for computer scientists). The ACM digital library reached 47,000 subscribers in 2001, more than 1/3 of the ACM membership (some of these are getting a student discount). ACM paper subscriptions have dropped about 1/3; however they had been dropping anyway.

ACM was caught in a cycle of an increasing number of CS researchers wanting places to put their articles, stimulating the creation of new journals, and spreading the readership ever thinner. ACM found itself printing more articles but fewer copies of each one as the membership distributed its purchases over the additional publications. With luck the digital library will be a partial answer to this since there is no problem with "small production runs" — articles of interest to only a small specialised group (such as the tenure committee at the author's institution) are just fine in digital form.

There was a time when Internet connectivity was free; there were services hoping to give away connect time in exchange for the right to send ads, or as a hook to sell more complex communications packages. These all died in the marketplace, and people now expect to pay for connectivity. Many for-sale online publications have died off also, after the hype of the dot-com boom collapsed. Yet, there are now some hopeful signs. A survey of the Online Publishers Association reported in the New York Times on August 1, 2002 estimated that consumers spent $675M on digital goods and services, with 12.4M people paying for some form of content.

Business and financial sites collected $214.3M. The total content sales in the first quarter of 2002 were $300M, almost as much as in the first half of 2001, which means that the area is growing strongly. On balance the subscription model for individuals has not been strongly succesful. It appears that libraries, or some equivalent buying club, remain the most obvious method for people in universities and research institutions to get their information.

Transaction Payments

Buying all the parts for a car costs more than buying the whole car. Many publishers used to dream of selling individual articles and getting more money than for magazines. However, this hasn't worked out. Many newspapers now sell their back articles through Newsbank, for example, but with prices at $2.50 an article or more, usage is low. There are several possible explanations of why this business model has not succeeded:

1. the price is too high for the demand;
2. there is enough free stuff out there;
3. librarians and readers are risk-averse.

A price of $2.50 for a single article from a newspaper that may have cost 35 cents for the whole issue on publication day certainly seems high. Of course this is a small amount of money if the information is of commercial value, but not that many older news stories have great value. "Yesterday's newspaper is like yesterday's fish," an old saying goes. There was a substantial effort in the late 1990s to develop "micropayment" systems. These would have been able to charge a few cents for things efficiently; First Virtual was perhaps the best known. None of these seem to have caught on. First Virtual Holdings started in 1994, became MessageMedia in 1998, and was acquired by DoubleClick in 2002. Cybercash also began operations in 1994 and was bought by Verisign in 2001 as part of a bankruptcy auction.

A sort of Gresham's law also operates because of the amount of free information on the web: why pay for a newspaper article if some free site will provide what appears to be the right information? Few newspapers have the kind of wide-spread name recognition that will cause people to seek them out (the New York Times, of course, being the best known); magazines with general public credibility are even rarer. Book publishing on the web for downloading is also a much hyped but little used methodology. In 2000 Stephen King tried publishing a book online in installments as shareware (payment on the honour system), with a threat to stop providing new chapters unless 75% of the downloaders paid for it. He quit after six chapters, claiming that only 46% had paid for the last installment, with about 40,000 copies sent out. Few other e-publishers sell any comparable numbers.

There was a rash of "e-book" publicity and products in 2001, which has died in the marketplace. Whether it will return when better devices with larger screens and lighter weight appear is unknown. In addition, many parties in this transaction are risk-averse, and don't like the uncertainty of buy-by-the-item. Journal publishers, for example, have traditionally avoided many conventional business problems by collecting in advance for subscriptions. If the check bounces, you just don't send the magazine.

You get six month's float on the money, and you don't need elaborate record-keeping to send out bills. By contrast, selling individual stories carries a need to count usage, compute bills, and chase down customers who don't pay. On the buying side libraries often get their budget once a year and don't like setting aside money for bills which can not be accurately estimated. Users are also often leery of expenses that can mount up quickly. All these considerations push the business away from pay-per-item and towards pay-per-month. It seems unlikely, therefore, that the eventual support of digital libraries will come from selling individual items by the byte. Perhaps the comparison is to photocopy machines: yes, there are a few of them being used in libraries with coin slots, or similarly in shops like Kinko's, but the bulk of the photocopy machines sold are in offices or homes and are not selling a per-page service.

Author-pays

Years ago Brown and Traub argued that page charges, assessed against authors, would greatly help the finances of journals. By collecting the initial cost of each page from the author, and the incremental costs from the reader, the journal would be economically secure as the number of subscribers or pages changed. Since the incremental cost of papers posted online is virtually zero, the idea of assessing all costs against the authors is attractive. In fact, that's what happens today — most websites are paid for by the author's employer. Should that be institutionalised in some way, with professional journals charging the authors to pay for their websites, and then not caring who reads them?

Page charges, however, were not a success in the scientific journal field. Many authors, given the choice of professional society journals with page charges and commercial journals without page charges, were happy to publish in commercial journals (which in some cases also offered faster publication or a better chance of having the paper accepted). It may well be that any money saved on page charges was paid back double in subscription fees, but that was the library's problem, whereas page charges usually were paid by the department or research grant. Since the authors route the papers to the journals, it seems likely that the same problem would reappear in the digital world.

Frequently, the organisers of meetings on this subject suggest that "authorities" impose rules on where scientists can publish. They may appeal to university presidents, government funding agencies, or whoever for a rule that requires publication in professional society journals or online. The practicing scientists are likely to resent such rules, however, and they are politically difficult to impose; university presidents have enough trouble telling the faculty where to park their cars, let alone where to publish their papers. An economic solution is almost certain to be more effective, appealing to the author's self-interest.

For example Steve Lawrence of NEC showed that online articles are cited more often than paper-only articles. Perhaps this may motivate authors to go to self-publishing on the web in the future. Unfortunately scholarly respect is not the same thing as actually being read. Remember the famous quip "deans can't read, they can only count"; the increasing length of scholarly monographs have led some to say "deans can't read, they can only weigh". Another problem with page charges is the shifting of costs among institutions. Although we tend to talk about the "scholarly community" and suggest that the readers and authors of journals are the same people, it's not a perfect match.

In particular, for scientific journals, there are both university and commercial organisations providing papers and subscriptions. The universities provide a larger share of the papers than they do of the subscriptions. Thus, shifting costs from readers to authors would shift costs from commercial organisations to universities, and the universities are probably less able to bear the burden. A large part of the difficulty is with prestige. Authors of scientific papers normally publish for credit, promotion and renown, not money. It has proven difficult to persuade authors to send their best papers to an online journal; they fear not being suitably rewarded during tenure decisions, for example. It ought to be possible to quell such fears by using the prestige of either major universities or major scientists.

So far, unfortunately, the tenure committees and university presses have been even more conservative than the faculty in general and the most desired publications are still on paper, even if the ones most read are on the Web. Despite this history, late 2002 saw a major new effort in the biomedical area to create an online journal funded by page charges, the Public Library of Science. Several major scientists, including Harold Varmus, are supporting this attempt to create an online journal with the prestige of Science, Nature or Cell. The Gordon and Betty Moore foundation has provided $9M of initial funding, and the first two journals, PLoS Medicine and PLoS Biology, should appear in 2003. Each article is expected to pay $1,500; funding from the Soros Foundation is available to help authors in countries where this charge might be prohibitive. Reading, downloading or printing the journals will be free. Time will tell whether this attempt will succeed.

Advertising Pays

Although advertising has rarely been important in the economics of scholarly journals, it certainly determines the financial health of more popular publications and of broadcast television. Is it possible that advertising could support digital libraries? There's certainly enough total money out there. Just to look at some minor categories, cable TV advertising and Yellow Pages advertising in 2000 were each over $12B. Online advertising, although smaller at about a third of that, is still comparable to total university library budgets.

There is wide disagreement about these numbers; the historical statistics below are from the Internet Advertising Bureau and the future predictions come from firms such as Jupiter and Forrester.

The market for Internet advertising has been stagnant of late. The most recent quarterly report, showing $1.47B of ads in the third quarter of 2002, was a 1% advance on the previous quarter and an 18% decline from a year earlier. Online advertising has been dropping for six quarters, partly because so much of it was placed by other dot-coms which no longer exist. Advertisers have become discouraged as fewer than 1% of people who view an ad click on it. Unfortunately, despite the $4 billion total (or more), it's all focussed on a few websites, particularly the very popular ones.

The potential for specificity in web advertising is not used as fully as it might be; few sites other than the leading search engines and portals get much advertising. It is hard to imagine enough advertising going to libraries to make a difference. Even in the boom years most small journals, for example, did not attract many ads to their websites, and it is unlikely that libraries, even if they sought out ads more actively, would get many. As the Internet advertising market has matured, the ad placement has gone mostly to a few heavily used sites.

Thinking historically, very few scholarly journals got a large fraction of their budget from advertising, with only a few ads for books and employment positions on their back pages. Libraries have not historically sold advertising, and have not seen much opportunity there. The main "advertising" in a library has traditionally been for donors: buildings, reading rooms, and book purchase funds are named for individuals the way sports arenas are named for corporations. And one problem with computer technology is that its transitory nature and the rate at which it becomes obsolete make donors reluctant to fund it, since whatever their name is on may evaporate in a few years. On balance it seems unlikely that digital libraries will find much advertising support.

Other Possibilities

Grant support: The Andrew W. Mellon Foundation is particularly well known for its funding for activities such as JSTOR and ArtStor. JSTOR, having been started with Mellon funding, is now an independent not-for-profit institution. Although many other foundations (Kellogg, Soros, and the Packard Humanities Institute come to mind quickly) support libraries, it is not reasonable to expect that operational funding for digital libraries will come from these sources. Some projects are supported by government funding (in the US, typically the National Endowment for the Humanities or the National Science Foundation), but again these tend to be specific research projects rather than long-term support.

Cost avoidance: Many companies have gone to putting information on websites as an alternative to customer service operations. Similarly, much material intended at least partly as publicity or advertising, even if traditionally sold, may well be placed on websites. For example, you can buy the San Francisco Muni Transit map for $2.50, or you can find it on the Web for free. The transit system's finances are based on ridership, not map sales, and they are happy to provide free access to information as a way of encouraging transit use. Similarly many government agencies now publish their information on the Web rather than, or in addition to, printing it on paper; in general these agencies were only trying to do cost-recovery anyway. Some professional societies may turn to free online distribution for similar reasons. This argument, of course, will not apply to commercial publishers.

Advertising the print medium: The National Academy Press has, for a few years, been putting all their new books on the Web for free access, and providing the complete text of each book. To the surprise of many, the result has been an increase in their print sales. Similarly the Brookings Institute has put 100 of its books online free, and the paper sales of those books have doubled. This result is perhaps similar to the experience of record companies, which found years ago that having their records played free on the radio increased disk sales. In fact, recording companies were willing to slip cash to disk jockeys to select their records, producing occasional "payola" scandals.

Web availability has encouraged readership of out-of-copyright items as well. The University of Virginia is distributing almost 7 e-books a minute, with more than 6 million shipped so far (in the first 21 months of operation). Perhaps it is not surprising to see "Alice in Wonderland" and "Huckleberry Finn" near the top of their "best-seller" list; but in one month they sent out more than 2000 copies of the works of Andrew Dickson White. One wonders if he sold that well during his lifetime (although he was President of both Cornell University and the American Historical Assocation in the 19th century).

Index